THE GOOD SOLDIER

Conscience, Committed, Consecrated

A Clarion Call to Prayer

Featuring a memoir of Eddy Johnson, a US Army
"Desert Storm" Veteran

Dr. Purity M Williams

Publishing Coordinator – Sharon Kizziah-Holmes

Published by

An imprint of:
New School Bus Creation Music, Ministry & Publishing LLC
Springfield, MO

ISBN -13: 978-1-960499-43-1

ACKNOWLEDGMENTS

For me, there is no life without the Life-giver, Yeshua (Jesus) Christ. He is Lord, Savior, and Restorer. Thank You my Lord for another chance to walk in Grace, Truth, Destiny and Your glory.

Mr. Eddy Johnson, thank you for your participation in this writing. I am blessed and grateful for your journey and the testimony of Jesus in you. Many thanks for your dedication to God and service to our country.

Apostle Cornelius & Mrs. Tina Perry, (and remembering the late Pastor Patricia Shackleford); great leaders are not easily found, and you are of the greats in the earth. Your love, life and ministry inspired this writing. I love you, and Apostle, thank you for your faithful service to our country.

Jin, Frederick, and Sara, my loves, I am so grateful to God for you, my children, and to be your mother. I love you and see you as powerful leaders in the earth.

Many thanks and unending love to the special parents who raised me and love me, Pastor Johnny and the late Hattie Williams.

Aunt Rosie Akins and the late Aunt June Marie Webb (2023), you enrich us, and your lives and testimonies mean so much to our family. Thank you!

Glennis Munday, Wanda Stamey, Deb Sonnor and Linda Givens. I love you my friends and prayer warriors.

Photography—Carl & Helen Williams

Logo Manifest—Christopher Williams

Co-editing team with me—Wanda Stamey

Many many thanks!

And to Sharon Kizziah-Holmes, writers/authors have found a place in history because of your work. Thank you for your labor.

CONTENTS

INTRODUCTION

In the history of man's existence, the earth has witnessed mighty moves of God. Therefore, it should be understood that the Almighty loves His Creation. And it is in the times when men and women have sought His Face in repentance or to know Him, even His Hand, that He has shown Himself strong by His great Name and power.

From such, we see Enoch, who walked with God and eventually the Lord God took him out of this world because of their beautiful relationship (Genesis 5:24); to Noah, who found grace in the sight of the Lord (Genesis 6:8-9), built the ark while preaching to an obstinate people and was saved from the flood waters along with a few others (1 Peter 3:20); to Moses' mind-boggling encounters with the Lord, he was given the Law, and the grace of prayer and intercession to touch the heart of God on behalf of Israel, who constantly strayed. And it was noted in the scriptures that God spoke with Moses face to face as a man speaks with his friend (Exodus 33:11).

Hagar, the Egyptian bond woman was the one who experienced the Lord as the "God who sees" (El Roi) (Genesis 16:13), and Ishmael, whom God heard when he was dying of thirst in the desert (Genesis- 21:17) after they had been dismissed from the camp of Abraham and Sarah; David was a man after God's own heart (1 Samuel 13:14), and when he sinned, he knew that it was the Lord he could trust to be merciful to him and not man.

To Daniel, who was a man of intense prayer and walked closely with God and was saved from the mouth of the lions (Daniel 6:1-22). To many others all the way to our Lord and Savior Jesus Christ, who redeemed us from our sins, iniquities and opened the door to eternal life and immortality for mankind again (2 Timothy 1:9-10).

And finally, to those who since the first coming of our Lord, have chosen to come to Him for salvation, renewals, breakthroughs, healing, deliverance, revivals and restoration…every single one of these people came to what I will call *"The Crossroads of Adjustments."* And every single one of them that faced their crossroads with prayer and trust in the Lord, received the victory.

Sincere and non-amiss prayer (James 4:3) is like a perfect communication into the heart of God. This is because this kind of prayer, in regularity, moves upon the heart of the Lord God to deliver a seed of His heart, if you will, that goes into the innermost part of the being. That seed produces after His kind. It yields life, light, and immortality within. It produces hunger and thirst for Him and for what is right. It promotes change. It allows the Mind of God to have His way. It allows for transformation into His likeness. It opens the door into the very Consciousness of the Highest to awaken in us as well as overshadow us. And it calls upon God and permits Him to set or fix His way and His patterns in us.

Thus, the Almighty has a marvelous way of revealing Himself in pattern. Even in the Garden, the Lord met with Adam in the cool of the day (Genesis 3:8). This was a faithful pattern of YAHWEH. It reveals His great love and desire to fellowship with His creation. He wanted the Man and the Woman He had made to know that He was their assurance and that they could trust Him. The Lord, Adam, and the Woman were in Covenant. Their consistent meetings together could be reckoned as prayer. And isn't it true that one does not know someone unless they have taken the time to learn them? Our Lord Yeshua (Jesus) said these beautiful words, *"Take my yoke upon you, and learn of Me; for I am meek and lowly in heart: and ye shall find rest unto your souls"* (Matthew 11:29). And if you read the passage of Adam's meeting place with God, (though it does not say this was a daily thing) you will see that both Adam and the Woman heard the *familiar* sound of the Lord walking in the cool of the day. Sadly, it is at this point in their narrative, that they had made a grave mistake and sinned against the Lord and their covenant with Him. They experienced something they had never experienced before...Fear. And they hid themselves from Him. It was never their pattern to hide from their loving Creator, but to embrace their fellowship and communion with Him when He visited them. Again, this was the Lord's pattern to come and fellowship with the Man and the Woman He had made.

This reminds me of something I learned from my leaders in North Carolina: *"The Almighty does not break pattern"* - *(Apostle C. A. Perry)*. However, humanity breaks pattern all the time. And as a result, we find it very difficult to trust each other. Please understand me! I am talking about breaking pattern that is right, reliable, and trustworthy. When we break pattern we move away from the place of safety and find ourselves in unfamiliar territory with God and each other. Even in a marriage when one of the spouses break pattern, red flags go up. When someone breaks pattern they have come to a crossroads. If the right decision is made, that person will see sooner than later what they were saved from. If not, that person's life will shift and take a spiral downwards and away from God and their true purpose. In that spiral, many things begin to take place. Additionally, this spiral will produce suffering, much of which was never intended to take place in that individual's life, but to our grief, sometimes is the only way a lesson can be learned of what is real, true and precious. And in the process of suffering, we can learn obedience.

Regretfully, along the way, our faith can take a beating and become stale or small. But if we cry out to God, the Lord is loving and merciful, and will diligently work with and in us to help us learn of Him so that our faith in Him can be restored.

I must tell you that there are side effects that comes as retaliation of our movements of error. To name two side effects, the 'hiding spirits' called, Guilt and Shame, find an open door in our lives when a great blunder has been made. They inwardly ride our backs like a two-humped camel, continually jabbing at our hearts and torturing our minds to remind us of our delusive ways. However, if we can find repentance, we might be able gain another chance to fulfill eternal purpose.

This is accomplished through the fellowship of *prayer*. We have such a perfect example in the Author and Finisher of our faith, Jesus, the Christ. I will also be using His Hebrew and Aramaic name, Yeshua, also called Iesu, Yehoshua and Isa (Arabic) throughout this work simply because it is His original name.

Moreover, another author said these faithful words in the Book of 2 Chronicles, Chapter 7:14:

¹⁴ If my people, which are called by my name, shall humble themselves, and pray, and seek My face, and turn from their wicked ways; then will I hear from heaven, and will forgive their sin, and will heal their land.

Prayer is the vehicle through which we can receive grace to walk righteously, to be, as well as remain steadfast, unmovable, effective, and faithful to our Lord, our fellow disciples and be light in a crooked and perverse generation. And like the good soldiers of the death and life of Christ, real prayer will help us to be studious, vigilant, alert, submissive and never break righteous pattern.

AN OUTLINE FOR THE GOOD SOLDIER...

2 Timothy 2:1-6

1. Thou therefore, my son, be strong in the grace that is in Christ Jesus.

2. And the things that thou hast heard of me among many witnesses, the same commit thou to faithful men, who shall be able to teach others also.

3. Thou therefore endure hardness, as a good soldier of Jesus Christ.

4. No man that wars entangles himself with the affairs of this life; that he may please him who has chosen him to be a soldier.

5. And if a man also strive for masteries, yet is he not crowned, except he strive lawfully?

6. The husbandman that labors must be first partaker of the fruits.

2 Corinthians 13:5

"Examine yourselves, whether ye be in the faith; prove your own selves. Know ye not your own selves, how that Jesus Christ is in you, except ye be reprobates?

Hebrews 9:11-14

11. But Christ being come an high priest of good things to come, by a greater and more perfect tabernacle, not made with hands, that is to say, not of this building;

12. Neither by the blood of goats and calves, but by his own blood he entered in once into the holy place, having obtained eternal redemption for us.

13. For if the blood of bulls and of goats, and the ashes of an heifer sprinkling the unclean, sanctifies to the purifying of the flesh:

14. How much more shall the blood of Christ, who through the eternal Spirit offered himself without spot to God, purge your conscience from dead works to serve the living God?

2 Timothy 2:10, 14-15

10. Therefore I endure all things for the elect's sakes, that they may also obtain the salvation which is in Christ Jesus with eternal glory.

14. Of these things put them in remembrance, charging them before the Lord that they strive not about words to no profit, but to the subverting of the hearers.

15. Study to shew thyself approved unto God, a workman that need not to be ashamed, rightly dividing the word of truth. kjv

CHAPTER (1)

The Grace Given to the Soldier

Thou therefore, my son, be strong in the grace that is in Christ Jesus. (2 Timothy 2:1)
Yeshua came by grace and truth because of the <u>sinfulness</u> of man, who was born into this world in a sinful state: of spirit, soul, mind and body. Yeshua came by grace and truth as the remedy because of our wicked state and the <u>sins</u> of humanity whereby we sin against God in our bodies. And He came by grace and truth because of the <u>consequences of our sin</u> (the three dimensions of sin by Mark R McMinn).

We cannot even begin to understand grace unless we understand the depravity of our humanity (Psalm 51:5-10). Many people are unable to grasp the concept of sin. The idea of sin is an inner force, and inherent condition, a controlling power, is largely unknown (Millard Erickson). Though *how* we were born into this world was not our fault, it is incumbent upon us that we seek to understand ourselves as to why we find uncomely things about us, wicked thoughts that plague us...even embarrass us, and acts that manifest out of us that are ghastly and beastly.

The Almighty knows we are a sinful people. And knowing our pitiful condition, He brought the solution. He bestows a unique grace on undeserving humanity that will lead us to an abundant life in Christ both now and throughout eternity. This unique grace brings us to enlightenment of our sinfulness and sins, a godly sorrow that leads us to repentance, and a justification before God along with sanctification as we grow in grace, wisdom and His character.

Walter Elwell, a biblical scholar gives a distinction between kindness, mercy and grace (all of which we need): a kind person is caring and gentle. Mercy is a particular sort of kindness; mercy is kindness to those *who do not deserve it*. Grace is a subset of mercy; grace is merciful kindness to those *who cannot deserve it*.

If I have found grace in your sight…

These are the famous words of Moses after the Lord had told Moses that He would not go up with him and the people into the land He had promised to them. But instead, would send an angel to drive out the people of the land. The Lord said this because they were a rebellious and stiff-necked people, constantly going astray (Much like us!) (Exodus 33:1-3). May we learn from our Sister, Israel and find the Way of escape. Moses interceded on behalf of the people and pulled on the grace that the Most High had bestowed on him so that God would not leave them, but go up with them. The Lord heard his cry. And then Moses asked the Lord to do something else for him. These are Moses words, *"Now therefore, I pray thee, if I have found grace in thy sight, shew me now thy way, that I may know thee, that I may find grace in thy sight: and consider that this nation is thy people"* (Exodus 33:13). Moses' heart was ever after the care of God's people and to accomplish the vision of the Lord to bring His people safely into the land of promise.

Additionally, we find that Bezalel, who was specifically called out by God, had to have the grace of the Lord God to do the work of the temple. It was said of him by the Lord in the JPS Hebrew-English Tanakh, "See, I have singled out by name Bezalel, son of Uri. son of Hur, of the tribe of Judah. I have endowed him with a divine spirit (the Holy Spirit) of skill, ability (grace), and knowledge in every kind of craft (Exodus 31:1-5). God is the God of grace, truth and excellence. And just as Bezalel had to be endowed with grace to do the work of the Lord, so do we in all our calling and election.

The New Covenant brings with it the divine staples of grace and truth. These are necessary parts of our salvation. The Law was given by Moses, but grace and truth came by the Lord Jesus, our supreme example (John 1:17). And if we can receive what He did, by grace we can live out a life of faith, trusting in what He did, and knowing that as we daily yield our bodies (members) to Him, He is working in us His will. He is working in us the holy life that is free from sin and condemnation. But if we err, or fall, we do have an Advocate, Yeshua Christ the Righteous.

For sure, I have found myself in various places where I needed the Lord's grace. In one particular place, I did not have family around or near me. In fact, there was absolutely no one but the Lord that I could confide in. It was a dark, lonely and desert place in my life, and I did not feel welcome where I was. But I knew I would be there for a little while longer. I remember CRYING OUT to the Lord to grant me His grace and mercy to continue. The hardships did not cease, in fact, they increased, but grace was imparted to me and eventually that chapter of my life came to an end. Truly, God is the God of all grace! (1 Peter 5:10).

The term that is most often translated "grace" in the Old Testament is the Hebrew word, *Chen* [Strong's 2580]. It simply means, grace or favor. And is mentioned approximately 66 times in the Old Testament. Furthermore, the Greek word for grace is *Charis* [Strong's 5485]. It is mentioned about 154 times in the New Testament. This word denotes a show of kindness, benevolence, favor, or a benefit given to someone. Grace is a gift of God. Additionally, it is a power, and an ability given to hear His call, truly *see* our wretchedness, be godly sorrowful and turn from sin. That same grace then enables us to follow and learn of Him in daily living, and do His Will.

In a general sense, the grace or 'graces' of God come in many dimensions and touches the many facets of our lives. For instance, in the Book of Romans Chapter 5:1-2, it talks about how the Believer in Christ Yeshua has been justified by faith. This justification is a grace of God. Britannica defines justification in Christian theology as either (1) the act by which God moves a willing person from the state of sin (injustice) to the state of grace (justice), (2) the change in a person's condition moving from a state of sin to a state of righteousness, or (3) especially in Protestantism, the act of acquittal whereby God gives contrite sinners the status of the righteous. Accordingly, the term, justification is a translation of the Greek dikaiōsis (Latin: justificatio), originally a technical legal term derived from the verb "to make [someone] righteous."

In the first verse of 2 Timothy, Chapter 2, Paul, the Apostle admonishes Timothy to be strong in the grace that is in Christ Yeshua. In one of our New Jerusalem Church services this year (2023), Pastor Perry talked about being strong in the Lord. If a person's spirit is strong, they can endure the trial, the suffering, and persecution, but if the enemy has been able to break their spirit, they cannot endure and may die from it. A broken spirit dries the bones (Proverbs 17:22), it dries up the hope we have. So, Paul is discerning and encourages Timothy in this manner.

One might ask, "Who was Timothy in regards to Paul the Apostle? Well, Timothy became a student under the tutelage of Paul's ministry and served with him (Philippians 2:19-22). It is believed that Timothy served as a scribe and helped Paul in the writings of several of the books we read in the New Testament today (2 Corinthians,

Philippians, Colossians, 1 & 2 Thessalonians, and Philemon). Timothy was born to a Gentile father and a Jewish mother (Acts 16:1). Timothy knew the holy scriptures from his childhood (2 Timothy 3:15), but it is a common belief that Timothy was brought to salvation under the ministry of Paul during Paul's first missionary journey. It is also believed that Timothy's grandmother and mother, Lois and Eunice, came to salvation during Paul's first missionary journey. They were highly regarded by Paul as beloved godly women of faith (2 Timothy 1:5). Thus, Timothy eventually joined Paul in most of Paul's second missionary journey after he left Lystra (Acts 16:1-5) and continued with Paul into his third missionary journey. He was later ordained with the laying on of hands by the presbytery to serve as a minister of the Gospel with Paul (1 Timothy 4:14). Timothy also ministered in several of the New Testament churches (1Thessalonians 3:1-2, 1Corinthians 4:17, Philippians 2:19-22, Acts 17:14 and 1Timothy 1:3).

When an individual is placed into the Body of Christ, and they follow Him, they are positioned in the Body as the Lord sees fit (1 Corinthians 12:18). This is also a strategic military move on God's part. Moreover, it is always a place where they will be profitable to the Kingdom of God and to mankind.

In the world, as soldiers goes through the process of their military journey there are benefits that are afforded them simply because they are a part of a branch of service. Likewise, the soldier of the Lord has benefits that are afforded to them simply because they belong to God's Kingdom (Matthew 6:33); (Philippians 4:19). Also, in the world, the soldier goes through these processes in hope for a life that will land them in a position of security and greater prosperity for them and their family. Some will get exactly what they expected or more, enjoy it with their family, while others' hard work and their life sometimes come to an unexpected end, and their benefits go to their grieving family.

Timothy, though young and sometimes intimidated concerning his youth, proved a loyal follower of Christ. He continued with Paul and matured into a faithful leader of the Ephesus Church. During Paul's imprisonment, Timothy was spokesman for Paul at Philippi and Corinth. It was said that he later suffered imprisonment himself. (Hebrews 13:23 may suggest to this). Sadly, Paul was martyred for the defense of the Gospel. *And according to tradition,* Timothy, Paul's son in the Gospel (Philippians 2:19-23), continued the work assigned to him as the governing Bishop of the Ephesus Church ([Eusebius] HE 3.4.6). However, the scriptures does not seem to communicate this information, thus it is safe to say, as Steve Burchette says in his article (in Christian Communicators Worldwide), that Timothy served from Ephesus as his base city, and was an *apostolic representative* and ministered under apostolic directives of Paul. This gave him freedom to move about and help minister to multiple churches in Asia. Quite some time later, according to Foxes' Book of Martyrs, Timothy was also martyred in 97 AD. for upholding the Truth of the Gospel he had poured his life into.

This marvelous grace is to be desired more than silver or gold. *For it is by grace that we are saved through faith; not of ourselves; it is the gift of God; not of works, let anyone should boast* (Ephesians 2:8-9).

Foxes Book of Martyrs speaks of the devastating cruelties against the saints before our time. Can you imagine the things that those who went before us suffered for this Gospel/salvation we sometimes take so lightly? Oh, how some have suffered! Some were stoned, some were sawn asunder, tempted, and slain with the sword (Hebrews 11:37). During the first century, followers of Christ were thrown to the lions in the Roman Coliseums for their faith. Some were tormented, some were burned at the stake, some were burned while their bodies served as street lamps at night and some were placed on large hot irons to be melted down. Only grace! ONLY the strength of the GRACE OF GOD can give a person the power to endure this kind of adversity.

I encourage and admonish us to cry out for His grace on a daily basis. I pray that we might consciously position ourselves to receive it for our whole life journey. We serve a God who is full of mercy and grace. Even His Throne is called the Throne of Grace and we can approach the Living God boldly through the shed blood of Christ, and find mercy and grace to help in our time of need (Hebrews 4:16). We may not know what we might have to endure for His name, but He will supply the empowerment of His strength, grace and power to go through it, glorifying Him. Moreover, we can let down our anchor of trust in this grace that has brought to us so great a salvation.

CHAPTER (2)

A Soldier Named Eddy Johnson

Eddy Johnson... (Personnel Administrative Specialist NCO)

When an individual enlists into a branch of service, they are accepting numerous responsibilities and challenges. After the "red tape: process of their induction, soldiers first must be put to the test through a form of 'Boot Camp' to discover areas they are strong in as well as weak, or need improvement. Unfortunately, as well as sometimes happily, there are those who go into a branch of service's Boot Camp only to come to the conclusion that a career in the military is not a good fit for them. And think about it, we find different types of boot camps in most every profession. In some places, they call it 'probation', other places call it 'apprenticeship', 'trainee', or 'novitiate'.

However, just because a person may find the military to be an unsuitable fit for them, they may not be able to just ship out and go home immediately. Within the first 180 days of active duty, the Army command may release a soldier without penalty by virtue of entry level separation, if the Army deems there is good reason to let them go. There is another way the Army can release their subjects from duty: it is through the (DEP) or Delayed Entry Program. This is where they give the individual a year to report to duty. Therefore, when the person signs their enlistment paperwork, *they* set the date when they will be called for their basic training. This will also give them time to get their affairs in order. Furthermore, being in the DEP segment gives the individual a door where they may able to back out of their enlistment. But they are responsible to contact their commander of recruiting for their area by mail. And their letter should say that they don't want to go on active duty and that they cannot be persuaded otherwise. They should state all their reasons for not wanting to go into the military. And even though the military is not obligated to accept their request, because they have not invested very much in the person at this point, the person most likely will receive a retraction letter.

On August 1, 2022, I had the honor of interviewing an Army veteran, Mr. Eddy Johnson (Personnel Administrative Specialist NCO), in his and his wife, Mrs. Sherra Johnson's home. Mr. Johnson is an example of the grace of God at work in the soldier's life. I asked him to share with me his journey as a military person. Later, for the truest clarification, he wrote a very condensed narrative of His 10-year tenure. Here is his story:

A Soldier Named Eddy Johnson

Where do I begin? I'll just begin with my arrival at the St Louis MEPS Station on 26, July 1987. It was a regular day, although I felt as if I was leaving something behind me as I was going up highway 67 from Poplar Bluff to enlist into the US Army. When I arrived at the MEPS Station in St Louis, I was just as lost as every one of the other recruits. I walked into the Station and then was shown my room where to put my bag. I only had one because I knew I was about to be transformed into another person. Immediately, the process of transforming into military life began. I was taken for physical exams and to sign papers. After my day was over I went back to my room not knowing what was next. But the next thing was 'chow' and sleep. The next day there were more examinations and papers to sign. That went on for the bulk of the next day until about 5pm. We then were taken as a group into the swearing-in room to take the Oath that locks you in as a soldier. As soon as we did that, it was off to the races, to Basic Training in Fort Knox, Kentucky. We arrived on the 27th of July at about 7:30 pm. Mind you, everything was rush, rush, hurry, hurry. So, we got off the bus in front of a hall of some sorts, went inside after the Drill Sergeant gave us a 'chalk talk,' informing us that we have arrived to the US Army Training Base at Fort Knox, Kentucky, and that we were no longer civilians but U.S. Soldiers. They then ushered us into the hall, sat us down and we received several blocks of instruction as to the dos and don'ts from there forward. After that part was done we were marched to chow and our barracks at the reception station. We were there for the remainder of our time at the reception station, a whole week or so. A lot of the training at this point consisted of basic stuff like shine your shoes make your bed, clean the barracks and how to do 'police call;' that is, how to pick up trash from the ground. There is a certain way they pick up trash from the ground: They line up in a line spread out and they slowly go through the field only picking up what's in front of you or on the sides of you. Very cool!

After my time at the reception station in Fort Knox, we were shipped to our unit to begin Basic Training. Basic Training began with showing us how to set up our wall lockers to 'Army Specs'. Shoes lined up underneath the bed. Clothes placed in the locker a certain way etc. Then we were told to get in our PT gear to start Physical Training, push-ups, set ups, running etc. We ran two miles every morning, and afterwards did all the rest of the drills. LOTS and LOTS of push-ups all day long. Intermittently. Everywhere we went we had to be marched as a company. We were never allowed to go anywhere alone. I was one of the oldest in my unit, so naturally, it went a little harder on me than the young'uns. But I was more physically fit than a majority of them.

So, we were trained on certain things by a schedule. For instance, today you learn customs and courtesy. The next day would be First Aid. The next day would be fighting technique and the next, drill and ceremony. Then the next day, how to take a M16 apart and put it together and so on and so forth. At some point we had to complete a 12-mile road march in full gear. Now, that wasn't easy at all. In Fort Knox, there are two hills that are steep. One called, 'Misery' and the other 'Agony' because that's what you felt going up and down these hills in full gear. I made the first trip. But the second one I failed at. They had to pick me up in an ambulance because I was about to pass out! When we went to 'chow' we were marched there as well, and given only ten minutes to eat. And we had to eat 'doggishly'. After lunch we would have more classes. We did PT or Physical Training morning and evenings. They would make us do so many push-ups till it felt like we were pushing up Fort Knox!

Our training came to the point where we had to go to the woods or Field Exercise. It lasted three days. We played war games out there. And I got killed every single time we did them. It was hot out there too because it was August. At some point we went to the gas chamber where we had to take our masks off and whiff the gas. It was so strong! Guys were coming out throwing up, face full of tears, falling down, and can't breathe. It was very hard on us. But it was to let us understand the seriousness of a mask and to trust it. We were allowed to go to the Chapel on Sundays. But at 12 noon we were back training. We had to pass a Physical Training test in order to graduate from basic. I scored 3rd highest in the group. When we had the Obstacle Training course, I didn't make it through the climbing the rope part. It was too high. My arms gave out.

But finally, I made it through Basic Training and was ready to ship out to AIT. This is where I learned my Human Resources position. I was sent to Indianapolis, Indiana for nine weeks. I enjoyed many parts of it. We were given passes every weekend. But I only used my passes two times. I have a nephew who lived there and I would go to his house. AIT was basically the same as Basic, but with less physical training and more freedom. They had a club there on post. I would go on weekends and "Get funky with it!" It was fun! Dancing and drinking and just partying. There was nothing special about AIT, just more training. But the food got better! We could go to the snack bar and buy our own food if we wanted to. There was a pool, we could bowl and play other games. I always got the chicken and hamburgers.

After graduating from AIT, I went on leave for two weeks. Then I was shipped to Germany, which is where I experienced so much stress it was unbelievable! It was a nine-hour flight from St Louis to Frankfort, Germany. I experienced a lot of turbulence on the way. It felt sometimes like the plane was about to be thrown out of the sky. But we landed safely in Germany around 1pm. It was cold and new. They marched us over to the Military Reception Station and gave us our orders. Then we waited for them to put us on a bus to our unit.

I was then sent to Baumholder; one of the worst units in Germany. It was high up in the mountains. I got off the bus and they took me to my barracks, where I would live for the next two years. Then they took me to the Mess Hall and there I met a soldier named, Maclaine. We called him Mac. He asked me what I was doing that night, for it was New Year's Eve. I told him nothing, because I had just got to Germany and I had no money. So, he told me to come over to his barracks and when I got there he gave me $50 and some liquor. I was shocked because he didn't know me. But later on, I found out that that was the way it was in the Army. Everybody is close-knit. After that, I went to my room and settled myself in.

The next day I went to PT and First Formation and then on to Head Start for two weeks. In Head Start they taught me about Germany and some things to expect. They taught us some key German words like, how to ride the train, money and basic stuff. After my two weeks, my assignment kicked in. I was issued my TA50 (Field gear) and sent to my job. The first day was cool. But every day after that was hell. I started off as a SIDPERS Clerk. Computers and transactions etc.... hard stuff. I wasn't so good at it and I kept making mistakes. Seemed like I couldn't get the hang of it. So, my NCOIC started giving me the blues and a bad name. I became the door mat for my whole office. They treated me bad and tried to make me feel like I was stupid and dumb. They wrote me up and threatened to kick me out of the Army. I had so much sadness behind that because I knew I was better than that. Then they took me out of that job and sent me to the promotions area. But, by the time they moved me around I knew my job better than anybody in the office. I became the very best at everything. What they did was made me the best by treating me that way, because it made me determined to show them wrong. I was so good I didn't even believe myself.

For some reason, whenever the unit went to the field, I never stayed more than three days...ever! But those days were hell too. Cold and boring because not much of anything took place in the field. I remember one time I was pulling Guard Duty at night and I was tired, cold and sick of that mess. It was 2am, and it had to be two (2) below zero. I was sent to my post and there was a ditch there. Man, I got in that ditch, zipped up my sleeping bag with me, and my 16 and went to sleep. I couldn't help it. It was too cold.

The mud was at least knee deep in Hoeffel's, Germany. It was that thick slushy mud. And I was always ready for chow. I stayed hungry. We were out there for three days. It was an Army Training Readiness Exercise where different unit Battalions would have War Games Simulations against each other. So, I went back to the rear and the stressful environment resumed.

A new Sergeant came, and he was named Eddy as well. He picked up where the others left off with stressing me out and being hard on me. He was only doing it because he saw others doing it to me. I became so stressed out until I would do above and beyond what I was required to do, just to try and make up for the misunderstanding of the way they treated me.

It was a regular exercise for us to go on Company Runs. I remember on one run we ran up and down hills I guess for two hours or more. I was tired. Everybody was. When we were finished everybody was blowing fog out their mouths like clouds and steaming like a steam iron. I was glad that one was over. We did that at least once per month. We had First Formations every morning. It consisted of head count and salute to the flag. The cannon would go off after the Army song every morning. When the cannon went off we had to come to attention and salute. EVERY MORNING, five days per week! They have a much-regimented way of taking attendance. It's almost like a ceremony.

Finally, I made E4 Specialist in Germany. It meant a major pay raise too. By now, at the end of my tour in Germany, I had become so proficient at my job that Sergeants were asking me how to do stuff. I mean I was on fire! *Heard me?* Nobody, nowhere, could touch me.

The time finally came for me to make a permanent change of station. My next Duty Station was Fort Riley, Kansas, home of the General Custer. It was an Infantry Unit of Foot Soldiers. Kansas is where things started getting better for me. I was assigned to a Support Battalion. A small unit of 150 men and women. This unit was coed and had coed barracks too. It was at this point that I began to enjoy the Military and my job. When I reported to the office I was assigned the SIDPERS Clerk position, the same job that I was being dogged out for in Germany. And I got down to business. I had to tear down the area and rebuild it again because the clerk before me was not doing it right. I made an impression on my boss and I was treated like gold.

Soon I got more rank and was put in charge of other soldiers, *one,* of which brought me much misery when it came time for IG inspection. This soldier didn't want to do any extra work to put her area on point. So I wrote her up and she got severely disciplined for it. That's the way it is when you're in charge and your subordinates won't obey military orders. By this time, I had gotten used to being a soldier and many of the tasks that I had to routinely do became easier. For instance, Physical Training three times per week, two-mile runs every morning along with other exercises, like sit ups and push-ups and mountain climbers etc. Here they served chow three times per day, which is a soldier's favorite time of day! Soldiers were fed well. We always had end of day formations, which if there was any other task to complete after hours, that's when we were instructed what else to do; like pick up trash or go to the motor pool (Garage) and attend to the vehicles.

My unit went to California to train in the desert every six months. But for the whole time that I was there I never had to go. I was left back to run The WHOLE office. Which was cool because by that time I had been to the field so much I knew what they were going to do out there. Plus, the heat in the desert and I didn't get along very well. So it was cool.

Everything was routine until the war broke out in Iraq. One morning I got up to go to Physical Training, and before I went to formation I turned on the TV and there I saw an Abraham's tank with its turret pointing upward. And they said Hussain had invaded Kuwait and that Fort Stewart, Georgia was already in the air on their way over there. When I got to formation, the First Sergeant gave us the news that we had been alerted to deploy. My whole attitude changed instantly to *"A hell I done got myself into!"*. Suddenly our mission changed and along with our regular jobs we had to prepare to deploy the unit. We did things like check all our equipment for its condition and painted the vehicles Tan. That's when all the military vehicles in the military were changed from Camouflage to Sand color. Today you seldom see military fighting vehicles anything but Tan colored. This is when I learned to pack tight in the truck the things we were hauling. Still today I can put lots of things in a vehicle or a bag because of that experience. We had to take lots of shots before we could deploy. Some of which made us sick. Not me though.

We had briefings almost weekly until we left. It took us

from August until December to get ready for deployment. Finally, the day came that we were to deploy. We went to the arms room to draw our weapons and NBC gear. We then formed in our usual formation area and marched over to the buses that would carry us to the Rally Point; which was a gym. Everybody got back in formation once in the gym. They gave us one final briefing. All the ladies/female soldiers were crying like babies. Some because they had to leave their kids. Others for other reasons. Me, I was just in disbelief and in a daze that this was the REAL THING! We got back on the bus and road to the airfield in Manhattan, Kansas to board a plane to Saudi Arabia. After nine hours in the air, our first stop was Frankfurt, Germany. There, we were allowed to take a shower, and freshen up and rest up a bit. I think we were there for four hours. Then, we got back on the plane. We flew over Egypt. And looking out the window I could see the country. It was at night. All the cities were surrounded by lights. All in a circle. I asked what that was and they said all the cities are built in circles. The next stop was Osaka, Japan. We were there for an hour or so while the plain refueled. The whole flight to Saudi took us 18 hours. Finally, we got to Riyadh, Saudi Arabia. Got off the plane and marched over to a supply spot where we were all issued five big bottles of water and five Meals Ready to Eat (MRE). When I got there, I expected to see some trees or something, but no trees. NONE! Just sand and palm trees. As we drove through on our way to Dhahran and our barracks, we went through several towns. They had mostly Shell Gas stations and some other businesses (Shell is big over there). So, we finally got to Dhahran. Our barracks were used for the 'projects' in Saudi, but I don't see how because they were like condominiums, marble floors, etc.

After having been there about two weeks, suddenly, I got really sick and had to be admitted to the hospital. It lasted two weeks. After that I was returned to my unit and the War started the same day that evening. Sirens went off. Bombs hit the Port, and we could feel the ground shake from them. About an hour into the war, the order came for us to take the Iodine pills and go to top level 4 getting ready for a Chemical attack. We were in that posture for about two hours. Later that night we rolled out! We drove all night. On the way to the battle field we dawned our NBC gear about five times, stopping each time for about two hours. It was hot in that gear, sweating etc., and I was wide awake the whole time, buck-eyed (or wide-eyed)! We got to our location, set up the tents and were issued our ammo and some more supplies. I rode on the ammo truck the whole war. Our food in the field were hot meals from the MFK (Military Field Kitchen) in the morning and MRE for lunch and hot meals for dinner most days. If not, it was more MRE.

As I said before, there were no trees in the desert. Just open range and some tumble weed. It had to be around 100 degrees in January because it was very hot. No dirt, only sand. And underneath that was hard sediment. We could only dig our foxholes about a foot or two deep. Every morning we had to stand to attention or go to our foxholes and pull guard duty from 4am to 6am. Just sitting there looking for the enemy because that's when they like to attack in the morning round dawn. I pulled lots and lots of guard duty. I had Wash Dishes duty and Burn Waste duty. Yes, burn human waste! And I smelled like it after I finished. It was because I was an E4 and below in rank so we had to do lots of the foot work: driving, cleaning etc. I remember every morning the F16's and Bombers would fly over our heads after a night of bombing Iraq. Where we were stationed, there weren't any Nomads yet, but they eventually showed up later in the desert. They were hungry and thirsty, begging us for both food and water. We decided we would throw some of our provisions to them off our trucks. I remember one day I was going to another camp to visit a friend and there came this roaring sound that kept getting louder and louder over my head until it sounded like a missile right over head. All I could do was duck and think about God. Later that night First Sergeant called us all into formation and told us that they were going to be dropping a 2000-pound bomb at a certain time and that if we heard the roar of it and felt the ground move, not to worry because that's what it would be. I guess they prepped us with that information so we wouldn't panic and go to looking for our guns and dropping down or something.

The day finally came that we were to go into combat. At that point, I had to man up. I was all the way in it. And I couldn't call Sterling or Rose Etta (my parents) now. I mounted the back of the truck, locked and loaded my weapon and away we go! The ride was kind of smooth because we went behind the mine sweeping equipment. Tankers were in front of us and beside us too. Everybody was behind the mine sweepers because the ground was saturated with bombs. As we rolled out I would see "body parts" where things had been blown up. The whole desert sounded exactly like it was a thunder storm going on. Thus, it has its name Desert Storm.

The first day passed by and we stopped to get some rest. Everybody had to dig a fox hole beside their vehicles for the night. I was very tired by then. I only remember half the night. I pulled my guard shift and then went to sleep while they pulled theirs. Morning came and we rolled out again. Lots of airplanes over head. It was a massive movement with many fighting vehicles and such. It was like we mowed them down. At the end of that day, we got to a place near Kuwait and parked. It was about 5pm. The sky was dark and soot was in the air. All I could see was the sun peering through the smoke because the oil wells were on fire. We were only about three miles from the fires while others were closer.

The First Sergeant called a formation and told us the war was over. It was over in three days. I collected so many souvenirs and put them all under my bunk with the intention to bring them home. I had helmets shovels, bags, Mess Kits, AK47's, and more stuff. But afterwards, I wasn't so thrilled with it, so I left them there. Now, I wish I had kept them. They are worth money to a museum. We camped out for about two weeks, then went back to the rear. The drive back was so exhausting. We drove all night. I was so tired I couldn't stay awake. I slept most of the way back. And could have gotten in trouble but I just couldn't stay awake. Once we stopped on our way back and a 'Bedouin' or desert dweller came up to me with a stack of Iraqi money. He said all this for $10. I passed on the offer. Again, I wish I would have kept the souvenirs. When I got back to the rear, the Red Cross gave me a letter saying Grandma had passed. But they wouldn't let me go home because she didn't raise me.

We stayed at the redeployment center for another two weeks and finally it was time to go back to the states. Yeah!!! It was most exhilarating for me! I don't remember boarding the plane, but I remember being on it. We watched movies, ate good and slept well. We stopped in Germany again to refuel for about two hours and back in the sky. It was an 18-hour trip.

When we got to Fort Riley, we had a formation the next day, and in three days we were cut loose to go where we wanted for two weeks. I 'kicked it' in Kansas for a couple of days, and then went to Poplar Bluff to see my family. I had lots of money and was spending like a loose cannon. I gave lots to mom, siblings and paid mom's car off, then I took her to Memphis to buy clothes. And I just enjoyed having made it through the war unscathed.

Then the time came to return to my assignment in Fort Riley, Kansas. But I would only be there for three months because before the war, I had reenlisted for Korea. When my name came down on orders to go, I was flown to Korea. We landed in Osun, South Korea about 9am their time. Then I received orders to go to Seoul, not knowing what unit I'd be assigned to. Well, to my surprise, I was assigned to Seoul. Lawd! Lawd! Until Seoul, I had had nothing but leg assignments. Leg Assignments meant hard duty in an infantry unit. In fact, I was 'tracked' for Infantry Units because I had so much experience with being in one. But they changed the game up and assigned me to a Vegetarian Unit—what we affectionately call the "Doggy Doctors." LOL! But they handled everything with USDA. I was assigned to them and attached to the Main Hospital in Seoul, South Korea. This was a plush, cushy assignment. After all, I had paid my dues. This assignment was the best in the world, I thought, until I got to Cleveland, Ohio. I was then assigned to the MEPS Station (Military Entrance Processing Station) as a PSNCO.

I arrived at Cleveland Hopkins Airport on 13th December, 1993 at 5pm. It was snowing and cold as all get out. It was my first impression with my new duty station— and it held up to its impression too. I saw some really bad winters in that city. Because it was a unit that was not on a military installation, it had its perks as well as draw backs. I no longer had the supervision I would have on a regular post nor the tasks to accomplish like Formations, Trash details, Charge of Quarters duty etc. It was largely like a 9 to 5 job as a civilian in military uniform.

From there, I caught a cab to the Red Roof Inn. There I stayed for two weeks until I found an apartment to live in— *all expenses on the Army*! I had no car then so I had to learn to ride the bus and the train to wherever I had to go. It was challenging to say the least, but I figured it out. I had to or else be punished for not going to work. LOL! Those rides to and from work in the winter time were cold and frigid because I had to wait at some stops to catch the bus to the next stop. Sometimes it was snow and 10 below. Then I had to wait for 20 or 30 minutes for the next bus. It was brutal! I arrived at my duty station and was given my assignment, which was to be a Personnel Sergeant in charge of my office and all personnel actions for the soldiers and military personnel assigned there. I was an E5 Sergeant when I arrived. They loved me because I knew my job so well and could really take good care of my folks. I had no subordinate soldiers to supervise. I ran the whole office myself. EVERYTHING! Then I came down on orders again after about 5 months there to go to BNCOC to prepare for my next higher rank, E6. They sent me back to Indianapolis for eight weeks. There, I learned the leadership responsibilities of my next higher rank. In BNCOC I had to learn how to march troops, supervise a whole office, field tactics, and more of my specific office duties as well. When I finished that, I was promoted after about two months to E6. And then I was in charge of all enlisted soldiers at the MEPS Station except the Master Chief, E9. They sent me to Fort McCoy, Wisconsin for more training in my specialty for approximately a week. It was cold up there! Ice cycles were coming off the mountains as big as a football field. Then I ended my term of service on the 5th, June 1996 at Fort Knox, Kentucky where it all started. This is where my military story ends.

Questions and Answers

I asked Mr. Johnson several questions:

Question 1: Did your perspective of God change during your 10-year military career.

Answer: Nothing really changed. I kept serving the Lord. However, during the great struggle I had on the job with my fellow department personnel and the man who was also named Eddy, I did get more involved with church and reading the Bible. I went to church sometimes at the Church of God and Christ (but when I was in Cleveland, I went to church a lot there). I finally invited Eddy to church, and he got saved! In my life as a Believer, that is the only one that I had a part in getting someone to the Lord. And that counts for something. Eddy did not hassle me so much anymore, but he *was* of higher rank than myself.

Question 2: What about your perspective on prayer?

Answer: When I go down in prayer, I don't pray for five hours, but I try to be sincere as I can. I never worried about food or anything like that because God feeds the birds and I believe He will always feed me. I pray often for wisdom and understanding and I want to know the truth and what God wants me to do. Now, when we were shipped to Saudi Arabia, I got real close to the Bible and God. I realized it could be imminent death and therefore I testified to people there about the Lord.

Question 3: What was the most rewarding thing about your career?

Answer: Getting on the plane from Saudi Arabia and coming home from the Desert Storm war. It was calculated that only 90% of the force or the first wave, (of which I was in), would survive. We were supposed to have died. And we were put on the front lines to hold the fort until the real soldiers came in. But we were the real soldiers. They did not have to send the other troops.

Question 4: Did you suffer from PTSD? And if so, what was that like for you?

Answer: Yes, I did. But it was mild. I didn't want to believe I had PTSD, but they ran several tests on me and each one revealed that I had PTSD. I don't like unexpected noises. Neither do I enjoy 4th of July, New Years, fire crackers any more. I also deal with road rage and anxiety like many other civilians.

The Meaning of Some of The Army's (Abbrev) Verbal Communication

Some of the military abbreviations that Mr. Johnson used may have been self-explanatory, however, just for the sake of understanding, here are the meanings of some of the various military abbreviated language:

MEPS—Military Entrance Processing Station. This is a facility which is staffed by service members from all branches as well as civilians. They process individuals who are looking to join the Armed Forces by medically, physically and morally screening them against Department of Defense Standards.

BCT—Basic Training. Consists of the first ten weeks of the total Army basic training period.

AIT—Advanced Individual Training. In the Army, AIT is the portion of the training cycle that takes place after Basic Training.

MRE—Meals Ready to Eat: These prepared meals can last a very long time. It is best to use by the 3rd year for freshness and nutritional value, however, they can last up to 10 years (some longer).

BNCOC—Basic Non-commissioned Officer Course. This is an 8-week training course for infantrymen that provides NCOs (Non-Commissioned Officers) with progressive and sequential tactical and technical training which is relevant to infantry Soldiers' duties, responsibilities, and missions which will be performed in operational units after completion of the course.

IG—Inspector General. The IG investigates and reports on the discipline, efficiency, economy, morale, training, and readiness of the army, and acts as the eyes, ears, voice, and conscience of the (SA) Secretary of the Army and (CSA) (Chief of Staff of the Army).

MFK—Military Field Kitchen or Modular Field Kitchen. This setup can, with assigned personnel can serve three hot meals a day for a 250 troops on a sustaining basis.

NCOIC—Non-Commissioned Officer in Charge. This officer is tasked with technical and organizational assignments critical to day-to-day operations and special operations.

PSCNO—Personal Staff Non-Commissioned Officer.

SIDPERS—Standard Installation and Division Personnel Reporting System (SIDPERS) was the main database or, rather, databases for personnel accounting by the US Army. The Active Army, US Army Reserve, and Army National Guard each had separate, largely incompatible databases, each bearing the name SIDPERS or a variation thereof.

AK47—Assault Rifle

Mess Kit—According to the Army Navy Warehouse article, the Mess Kit is a former staple of the US Military and often used by campers and survivalists. Although no longer an issued part of the Military Issued Field Gear since 2002 because of the MRE, the mess kit remains an iconic & functional tool in the mess gear.

Information for these abbreviations and meanings were mostly retrieved from online sources.

CHAPTER (3)

What the Soldier has Heard and Been Taught

We are a product of what we have 'caught' or been trained and taught.

The Apostles and disciples of Yeshua were taught by the Lord for 31/2 years. He not only taught them the word, parables and the way of eternal life, He sent them into clinical trials and allowed them to exercise what they had been taught. They experienced marvelous victories (Luke 10:17) and some failures (Matthew 17:16-20). Then the time came for the Lord to give His life. He died for us. He rose, spoiling principalities and powers, (Colossians 2:15) having defeated Death, Hell and the Grave (Romans 4:25). After He had risen from the dead and was seen by over 500 people (1 Corinthians 15:6), He gathered the disciples to Himself before His ascension that He might instruct them concerning what was about to happen. He commanded them not to leave Jerusalem until they had received the promise of the Father (Acts 1:4). He had already told them that He would not leave them comfortless since He was going back to the Father (John 14:18), but would send that promise to them (The Holy Spirit—Ruah HaKodesh). They went into the upper room where they cried out in prayer to God for that promise to be fulfilled. The Lord did not disappoint them. The Holy Spirit came like a rushing mighty wind and fire. And those disciples were endued with power from on high to continue the work of Christ (Acts 1:1-5); (Acts 2:1-24).

Those disciples/saints of old walked in Dunamis power. It was inherent because now, in the New Covenant, the Spirit of God works or specializes *within* the person, not just without, like He did with Samson and others in the Old Testament. There was a time when many were following the Lord (John 6:1-2, 24-65), but by the time He was going back to the Father, that bunch Yeshua taught, had dwindled to 120 in the upper room (Acts 1:12-15), and they received miraculously what they could never have done in their humanity.

When we look at the military branches, (Marine Corps, Navy, Air Force, Army, and Coast Guard), each of them has what is called, Special Forces that go into certain territories that other parts of the military are not equipped to handle. Those men and women from the upper room became like the special forces or 'sent ones' of the Kingdom of God. Now, the Lord can use whoever He chooses, but these men and women carried something that we must sometimes travail to breakthrough in prayer and intersessions, to have restored to us, the Body of Christ as a whole. We need the true leaders of God or the sent ones to help us in this restoration.

When I think of these soldiers in training, one of the main things that come to mind are the 'drills', (and sergeants screaming at the soldiers to do push-ups—forgive me, I am smiling as I think about the old series of Sergeant Carter and Gomer Pile). But in all seriousness, it is inconceivable for the civilian to really know what many of these soldiers have to endure in training to come to peak condition for their missions. Even the word itself, (drills) sounds 'excruciating'. Those drills are done over and over and over and over again until it is just a part of the soldier's life. Furthermore, there are a host of other things they are taught and trained to be ready in an instant for any unique or emergency situation.

Part of my training in North Carolina reminds me of drills because our leaders would repeat things again and again. It would never be exactly the same, like drills, but in different teaching slants so that our learning and *doing* can be optimum. It always had a freshness to it as if we are learning it for the first time. But as time passed, we began to receive enlightenment and recognize that the foundation was being laid and the truths had to be in place for our growth, that we might understand and walk out what we were being taught. If we grabbed hold of those things, we were successful because it took form in us so that we would be able to share it with (or disciple) others in the same spirit in which it was given to us. Mind you, though we may not say or demonstrate it quite the same, if we operated the ministry in the same spirit as we were taught, we would be assured we had understanding and the spirit of it. This is what Yeshua did when He took a motley crew of disciples and turned them into a force to be reckoned with.

In his book, "Jesus On Leadership," C. Gene Wilkes asked the question, "Why did Jesus need the disciples? Well, Yeshua came to carry out the Father's mission; which was to give His life as a ransom that as many as would receive His sacrifice would be reconciled to God. His mission required those who would join Him and become one with His vision and mission of reconciliation. Those who caught what He lived and taught, would in turn continue His mission, being equipped and "teamed" to carry it on.

By the same token, Paul the Apostle was very absorbed in discipleship. After his experience with the Lord on the Damascus Road, he was all about bringing people to the very One he initially rejected. For prior to Paul's encounter with Yeshua on that road and his conversion, he wreaked havoc on the Lord's Church against those who openly revered that name (Acts 8:3). In his madness against the disciples of Yeshua, Paul entered their homes, going from house to house dragging out both the men and women and throwing them in jail. He was also in agreement with those who killed Stephen (Acts 8:1). But when Saul (who was later named Paul) met the Lord Yeshua, it was like running straight into a brick wall while moving at 100 miles per hour. After this powerful Damascus road encounter, Paul sought God about what had happened to him. The Lord answered him by sending a Believer and follower of Christ named Ananias to lay hands on him, heal his blinded eyes and speak into his life the word of the Lord concerning the work Paul would do for God. Not long after this, Paul disappeared into the desert for about three years with God. When those years were up, Paul was ready to do anything, even lay down his life for the One who showed up, revealed Himself as the awaited Messiah, who alone could bring the salvation of God to the world. Paul wanted to learn of Yeshua, know Him and disciple others that they might know Him too.

Therefore, discipleship is of necessity; an inevitable course for one who desires a healthy spiritual life. It denotes people of different cultures and nationalities having a common bond, community and unity within. It is likened to a family, and has brought many a lonely person from having no kin to having a family that is learning to love like the God that saved them. These were Paul's words to Timothy, *"And the things that thou hast heard of me among many witnesses, the same commit thou to faithful men, who shall be able to teach others also" (2 Timothy 2:2).* He wanted those that came to the Lord to understand what they had received. They received the gift of reconciliation. They understood that it took a death to bring mankind back to God. They understood that it was not the blood of bulls and goats and heifers that would give them remission of sins anymore. They understood that this one Man's sacrifice would restore life and immortality to the walking dead. And when they were quickened from their death, they would run to tell others what great things the Lord has done for them (Mark 5:19). Paul taught diligently for their training/equipping and establishment in the Word, the Foundation, the Faith, knowing who their Heavenly Father is, who they have become, having believed in the Lordship of Christ, and their new citizenship with benefits (Ephesians 2:19-22). This was done for their sake and for the sake of those they would disciple. Moreover, just as our great U.S. military is in place to save the lives of American citizens, the soldier of the Lord is trained to bring people to the knowledge of the only Savior who can save the soul from eternal damnation. There is so much more!

CHAPTER (4)

Enduring Hardness

The good soldier of the Lord has been privileged to be in the ranks of the Body of Christ and called to grow into a supplying joint in the Body (Ephesians 4:16). Every member is to grow up into a soldier of the Lord in various degrees. And whatever the field of expertise, we are all soldiers.

In a Way of Life Literature study, David Cloud wrote about the Christian soldier. These are some of the distinguishing traits he described as characteristics of the Good Soldier:

1. The good soldier does his/her best—our utmost motive is to please the Lord.
2. The good soldier accepts his/her position—they don't choose their position. They don't even choose their gift and calling (God places us in His Body as He sees fit).
3. The good soldier follows the military rule book—for the follower of Christ, this is the Bible, studying self, and other relevant materials. We study and obey it.
4. The good soldier submits to authority and obeys orders—they have a Captain and leaders appointed by the captains. For the Christ Believer, it is the Holy Spirit, who lives in us, and the leader(s) the

Lord has placed in our lives who model love and obedience to the Lord.

5. The good soldier submits to military discipline. Discipline is the soul of an army. Our discipline speaks of our desire and movement to walk in the Lord's fullness.
6. The good soldier is dependable—God requires faithfulness in His soldiers because unfaithfulness causes hurt and harm.
7. The good soldier is a hard worker—laziness cannot be tolerated by the soldier.
8. The good soldier trains. Also, the soldier must be trained to be an instructor who can equip others.
9. The soldier fights—they learn their armor so they can be confident in the fight. We too have armor that we must prove.
10. The soldier endures hardness—enduring hardness and severe discipline is an essential part of soldiering.

The Power of Gentleness (the other side of hardness)

The **second** grade was a different year for me. At first, I was placed in a class with the homeroom teacher, Mrs. R. During my first-grade year, I would hear of how tough and mean of a teacher she was, and I was petrified of being placed in her class. Well, the thing I feared came upon me. Mrs. R. seemed short-tempered and mostly impatient with us. She did not smile often. And if you misbehaved or crossed her, you got the ruler to the hand. This reminds me of watching one of the old films of Jane Eyre (1983). In this film, a teacher, harassed a student named Helen because she did not like Helen. She thought of Helen as a dirty, disagreeable girl. (I must tell you, Mrs. R. did not harass me) But one day that teacher gave Helen several whacks to the hand with a long rod that she called "The

Instrument of Correction." I flinched while watching because I clearly remember what that felt like.

During my elementary years, corporal punishment was allowed in schools. I truly don't remember why, (maybe I was talking in class), but on one occasion I received the ruler spanking on my hand. I can still sense the pain of that experience. I felt helpless. From that time, I, who loved school, did not want to go back to school anymore. And I knew it would be difficult to continue in that classroom for the rest of the school year. I don't remember telling my parents about the incident, but something extraordinary happened. Somehow, (I don't know the reason), I was moved to another second-grade class—to Mrs. Crawford's class. To this day I remember her very clearly. She was the kindest of teachers and of people I had ever met. She was very gentle with all of us. She never raised her voice, yet she knew when to be firm. From this position of gentleness, she never broke pattern. And she was helpful in our inadequacies. She always had a smile and her temperament made it easy to excel in her class. Her spirit was so powerful that to this day I remember what it *felt* like to be in her presence. With her as our teacher, it gave us an advantage. I enjoyed school again and believed I could do well—even with the tougher areas of my education.

Gentleness is like an undercover prayer that tenderly makes its way into the heart of the individual. It is hard to resist it because it gives no cause to be alarmed or angry. Mrs. Crawford's gentleness was likened unto this and was born out of the Love that can heal the deepest wounds. It was a love for people, the love for souls. What she possessed was extraordinary and could have only come from God. 1 Corinthians, Chapter 13 tells us about love in this manner:

13 Though I speak with the tongues of men and of angels, but have not love, I have become as sounding brass or a clanging cymbal.

2 And though I have the gift of prophecy, and understand all mysteries and all knowledge, and though I have all faith, so that I could remove mountains, but have not love, I am nothing.

3 And though I bestow all my goods to feed the poor, and though I give my body to be burned, but have not love, it profits me nothing.

4 Love suffers long and is kind; love does not envy; love does not parade itself, is not puffed up;

5 does not behave rudely, does not seek its own, is not easily provoked, thinks no evil; 6 does not rejoice in iniquity, but rejoices in the truth; 7 bears all things, believes all things, hopes all things, endures all things.

8 Love never fails. (1 Corinthians 13;1-8 NKJV)

It is from this *Being* and power (Love) that we are able to do unto others as we would have them do unto us. It is from this power of love that gentleness is born and gives us the grace to give a soft answer when we are railed upon or tormented by others. This makes me understand gentleness as that which gives power to endure harshness because it is birthed out of Love. It is the power of love that causes our faith to work and allows us to receive the grace that is needed every day. And it is from the gentle heart of God the Father and the power of His Love that salvation came to us in the Person of Yeshua Christ. This is a true advantage.

We all learn differently. And for some people it takes having experienced Love—at least some measure of it, to be able to suffer and endure some things in life… and *not go rogue*.

Paul knew, even from his own experiences that Timothy would have to endure some very tough things. Even with following Paul, Timothy would have to deal with hardships... by association.

If you recall or have read about Paul and Silas, Silas, who like Timothy, followed Paul in ministry, suffered imprisonment. This story began with them walking along the way of going up to prayer. As they walked, a young woman who was possessed with a spirit of divination kept hollering out that Paul and Silas were servants of the Most High God, who came to show the salvation of God (Acts 16:17). After many days of listening to this woman say the same thing, Paul, being grieved, turns, rebukes and cast out the spirit from the woman in the name of Jesus and set her free. But unfortunately for her masters, she could no longer produce money for them through her now former ability to soothsay. They were enraged, reported them to the authorities, and had Paul and Silas cast into prison for messing with their livelihood. Paul and Silas were cruelly beaten and whipped, but it did not remove their joy and love for the Lord or to share the Gospel. And to the glory of God, the prison guard and others received the gift of salvation because Paul and Silas' joy, (singing praises and prayer in the prison), brought forth a miracle of God and the guard and others came to salvation. Because these men endured the hardships with patience and joy, others came to God through it (Acts 16:16-34). This salvation we are given is so very precious. But it did not come without a price. Yeshua paid a high price for us to be free; and on our journey we will not skate by without experiencing the hardships and persecutions that may follow us for serving Christ and refusing to live our former lifestyle (Timothy 3:12).

CHAPTER (5)

The Focused Life of the Soldier

In John Bunyan's Pilgrim's Progress, a man named Christian walked around with a burden on his back and a book in his hand. He would read the book, weep, tremble and give a sorrowful cry "What shall I do?" Christian often tried to share with his wife and children about the things he read in the book and the destruction coming to their city. But they thought he was delusional and was "losing it." Furthermore, the burden on his back was daily getting heavier and heavier. In Christian's prayerful desperation, the Evangelist was sent to him and gave him a letter and directions to the "Narrow Gate". As Christian made his way to the gate, he was met with those who tried to turn him back as well as all kinds of trouble (the Swamp of Despondence, Mr. Legality and the fiery darts of the wicked). But he was finally made able to enter in the Gate. On his journey within the Path, he was led to the Cross, where his burden (of sin and iniquity) fell from his back. In his rejoicing he was now on his way to the Celestial City (Heaven). However, from this place he was set to face a myriad of trials, tribulations, devices of the devil, and choices.

At the place called Vanity Fair, Christian faces forces pressing him to renege on his decision to follow Christ or receive imminent death. Though his friend is martyred, he stands strong. He thought he would also meet his end there, but escapes and his journey continues on. Truly everything about his journey from start to finish dealt with the seriousness and strong focus of the Path of Righteousness. Thus, the Christ Believer must be earnest, watchful, prayerful, kept by the power of God and given grace to maintain focus on our way to the beautiful Celestial City.

Both of my parents are unusual and gracious people. And there are unique expressions that came out of them. Daddy is a kind and generous man. He is an excellent and powerful singer. He is sweet, fun, joke-telling, hard-working and was committed to his pastoral duties. Daddy doesn't preach often now, but when he was at the height of his ministry, he was a great preacher and could hear God. People still gather around him to gain nuggets of wisdom from him. And he still has a way of talking to people that can make them melt.

I will always remember my late mother as a beautiful, smart, quiet, peace-loving, reserved, kind and most generous woman. Yet, before her conversion, Mama was not a person to play games with; she was no-nonsense, and her words were sometimes unfiltered and straightforward. After her conversion I watched the Lord slowly transform her. When the Lord called Daddy into the pastorate, Mama, in turn, became a pastor's wife, and had to learn to relate to people in ways she was not accustomed to. Her office of responsibility in the house of God forced her, who was a person who endeavored to stay in the background, to open up more, greet people, stand before them and bring messages of encouragement, as well as lead groups of women in her circle. As Mama grew in the faith and into her role, she began to blossom. I witnessed the grace of the Lord on her as she budded and matured into a virtuous woman, highly respected, whose words were like gold. Though she remained reserved in many ways and did not talk a lot on a personal level (unless you were very close to her), when she did speak, we would gather to hear what she had to say.

Mama always seemed to know what she wanted. She was focused. She went after the goal, and she got it. I will not forget that interval of my life where there was great turbulence for several years. My mother daily prayed for me. She sought God, among others for my safety and my life. She saw the results of her prayers. I am truly thankful! There have been occasions when I have felt stuck on my journey, but when in retrospect I looked back on her life, her challenges and many achievements, I was comforted and strengthened to move forward. To this day I cherish her; her fight (challenges she faced), her life (unique journey), and her focus (God and family).

2 Timothy 2:4 reads like this, *"No man that wars entangles himself with the affairs of this life; that he may please him who has chosen him to be a soldier"*.

When we hear that war is coming, we don't have to wonder if it will bring tough times. The presence of war always creates hardships. And the Christ Believer's life is sometimes likened to a war zone. The follower of Christ is dealing with their flesh nature that hates the Spirit of God that indwells them. There is a war (lesser or greater) every day in this fashion. This is only one of several reasons why a prayer life is of great necessity. And daily washing ourselves in the water of the word and learning how to meditate on the word will also keep our minds in a place of peace to deal with situations that come up in our lives.

The Lord God loved King David. He was a tender man, brave and a man of war. He grew up as a shepherd and related to the Lord as his Shepherd. At some point in his life, he wrote the powerful Psalm 23. He was the one that God acknowledged as, *"A man after My Own Heart"* (1 Samuel 13:14). David suffered many things simply because he had been chosen to be the next king after King Saul. For many years Saul chased David from place to place with the intent to kill him so he would not rule in his stead (1 Samuel 19-24). But the plan of God prevailed and David was made king of two tribes first, then of all Israel (2 Samuel 5:1-5). David was a focused man of war. He was good at what he did, and he was successful because he trusted in the Lord.

However, one day when David should have been out to war with his troops, he stayed back home. He ventured out on his roof, and across the way, saw a young and very beautiful woman bathing; he lusted after her. When he found out who she was (Bathsheba), he sent for her, and slept with her. She conceived and was with child. After she informed the king of her pregnancy, David devised a plan to put the pregnancy off on Bathsheba's husband, Uriah, the Hittite. Uriah was a faithful soldier of David's military force. David sent for Uriah to come visit him, fed him, got him drunk, and told him to go home and be with his wife. David later found out that Uriah did not go home, but slept outside of the king's house with the servants. Then David confronted Uriah as to why he did not go home and be with his wife. Uriah's words were piercing, *"And Uriah said unto David, the ark, and Israel, and Judah, abide in tents; and my lord Joab, and the servants of my lord, are encamped in the open fields; shall I then go into mine house, to eat and to drink, and to lie with my wife? As thou livest, and as thy soul liveth, I will not do this thing"* (2 Samuel 11:1-17). Though David tried that trick again, Uriah did the same thing; he went and slept at the king's door. Uriah's dedication and commitment to his king and to the Lord's army would not allow him to give himself that pleasure when his fellow soldiers were in such straits of war. Even drunk, Uriah's focus on war, on the king's business and his position was strong, and he could not be swayed otherwise. Furthermore, Uriah's faithful movements left David in an awkward, inner conflict of defeat. So, David decided to get rid of his faithful servant, Uriah. This decision would later cost him more than he could pay.

In her article called, "The Power of a Focused Life," Jen Roland wrote these words:

"Living A Focused Life Means...

Focusing on your PRIORITIES and learning how to eliminate distractions so that you can maximize your time and live in the moment. There are only two things on this Earth that are eternal – God's Word and people – so these two things should be at the top of your priority list. At the end of your life, it won't matter if you had a successful career, lived in a big house, or went on extravagant vacations. What will matter is if you chose to invest in those two things."

I appreciate what Ms. Roland has written, I believe this. And if I would say anymore to this, I would say that alongside what she has said, the priority of seeking the Lord in prayer will open us up to Him, make us empty ourselves of distractions and things of non-importance so that He has *room in us* to cause His word to come to life, as well as the need to invest that precious time with Him, in His word and people.

CHAPTER (6)

The Soldier is Lawful

And if a man also strive for masteries, yet is he not crowned, except he strive lawfully?
(2 Timothy 2:5)

Being lawful in simplicity means we are in accordance to the law. The online dictionary defines lawful as that which may apply to conformity with or in harmony with the law of any sort (such as natural, divine, common, or canon), the lawful sovereign.

During the kingdom of Darius, the Mede, Daniel was preferred over all of the other presidents and princes. Darius was minded to place Daniel over the whole realm because of Daniel's excellent spirit and how he immaculately handled the king's business. The presidents and princes were jealous and incensed over this and decided to find some kind of issue or problem with him that they might be able to put Daniel in a bad light or hinder his progress. Because Daniel handled the kingdom's affairs so efficiently, they could not find any fault in him; so, they went after Daniel's God (Daniel 6:5). They counseled together and concocted a royal statute in hopes that King Darius would approve and sign. The statute said that no one was to pray to any other god for the next 30 days, except to the king. If this law was disobeyed, that person will be thrown to the lions. This may have stroked the king's ego being considered a god, but for whatever the reason, he gave his signature. Now, once the king had established this statute and signed it, it could not be changed, revoked or altered according to the law of the Medes and Persians.

Directly after witnessing what these men did, Daniel left their presence and went to his chamber and place of prayer. He prayed three times a day as was his custom. Those men knew this about him. And mind you, the avenue of the Law of Daniel's God was the only thing they thought they might be able to use to come up with a plan to overthrow Daniel—and because their plan worked, for the time being it seems they had defeated him. They stealthily followed Daniel to his place of prayer and arrested him. As they brought him before Darius, the scales began to fall from the king's eyes; Daniel was the king's trusted adviser, subject and friend, and the king certainly was not willing that Daniel die. When he realized the craftiness of those men, he could do nothing about it. As king, he could not be unlawful. He was forced to uphold his own law. Daniel *had* to go the den of lions. And that meant that unless Daniel's God could save him, Daniel was going to die (Daniel 6). But God was indeed faithful to him, and pitifully, what those men intended for Daniel was heaped on them and their families. This was truly sad.

Our New Covenant causes us to know that the Law of God is written in our hearts and minds and we are given grace and truth in a divine new nature that we may live lawfully unto the Lord. We *are* in a race. However, we are not competing with each other. We are in a race where our flesh nature is continuously competing and warring against our divine one. Paul said this:

24. Know ye not that they which run in a race run all, but one receiveth the prize? So run, that ye may obtain. 25. And every man that striveth for the mastery is temperate in all things. Now they do it to obtain a corruptible crown; but we an incorruptible.

26. I therefore so run, not as uncertainly; so fight I, not as one that beateth the air:

27. But I keep under my body, and bring it into subjection: lest that by any means, when I have preached to others, I myself should be a castaway. (1 Corinthians 9: 24-27 kjv)

The word, 'castaway' is a very strong term. It means, "one regarded as unworthy, rejected; or rendered reprobate. Another interpretation for castaway here is this, "*that which is thrown away.*" It even goes on to say that that person is abandoned by God rendering them unworthy of His favor. This is a disturbing thought.

This makes me think of Simon the Sorcerer. He thought he could buy the gift of the Holy Spirit with money. But Peter, the Apostle sharply rebuked Simon, discerning the condition of his heart (Acts 8:9-24). For Simon had recently believed on the Lord Yeshua through the ministry of Philip. Simon even got baptized. However, as he watched Philip performing the signs and miracles of God, and witnessed the people receiving the Holy Spirit by the laying on of hands, he wanted that power...unlawfully. Thus, he was still in the throes of the same mind he had when he was bewitching the people as a sorcerer.

We often hear the name, 'hypocrite' given to a person who says one thing, but does another, who indulges themselves in the very thing that they speak against. In this sense, there is unlawfulness because their life is not adding up or balancing out. We as followers of Christ have been given a high calling. And to walk in it, our attention has to have a single focus that we may honor the God we say we serve. Remember, He works in us to do His will and good pleasure, but He needs our cooperation. The world laughs at the one who says they are a Christian but nothing about their life speaks of Christ. In this sense, the Believer gives the appearance that God doesn't care how we live. But He does care! And He cares for us. He cares for you. Moreover, our Christ life is not a *Que Sera Sera* (or Whatever will be, will be). We are not resigned to live out a life that gives us no victory over things that have plagued our lives. As we seek Him, we will know the truth of this.

We are in a world where on a daily basis this old nature has to be reckoned to the death whereby Christ put it to death. The old nature is most unlawful and cannot do right. It truly takes perhaps most of us a very long time to believe this. You may have heard someone reference another person as a *beast* because of their violence, the harm they do to others, or inconsideration of others. Well, if we really look inside ourselves, and are honest, we will see that our own humanity, in the worst of times and the best of times, can manifest itself akin to a beast.

I remember watching the famous original 1959 "Ben Hur" movie with Charlton Heston. After winning a most gruesome and brutal horse and chariot race, he received the grand award, which was an olive wreath commonly known as Kotinos (Greek: kotinos) composed of wild olive leaves (some have also called it a chaplet). This wreath was interwoven to create a circle or a horseshoe. It is said that the leaves were specifically collected from a holy tree called Kallistefanos Elea (also known as Elaia Kallistephanos). This tree was near Zeus' temple in Olympia, Greece.

In the Ben Hur movie there seemed to be no set rules for the races. They had no law there. And where there is no law, there is no sin imputed (Romans 5:13). Thus, the men who drove those chariots would not be judged, no matter how reckless or lawless their acts against each other. In this blood sport they had only so many rounds to make. And each contestant had to be on guard and watch out for the devious wiles of their fellow contestant, get ahead without being killed, and be the first to cross the finish line when the last round was made. And because there were no set rules, all was lawful and fair in the war of the races—including the deaths of the opponents by the hands of their competitors. Thus, in the ancient Olympics there were no gold, silver or bronze metals given to those champions. There was only one winner, and that winner received the Kotinos.

Additionally, I found that in 1896, Athens gave birth to the first modern Olympics. By this time, they had included several new events that had not been seen before such as: marathon, half-marathon, 100-meter sprint, 200-meter sprint, long jump, high jump, pole vault, round robin tournament, and team sports such as football and hand ball. Later, women tennis, and men's basketball were added, and then women's basketball started in 1952. To see these things in our day and time, I am in wonderment and greatly respect the hard work of the excellent athlete.

However, at certain moments in American history, the public began to hear of athletes who ventured into steroid usage to enhance their performances. For many years this was deemed unlawful for the Olympic athlete. Even while there were those who were disqualified after testing, the enhancement usage continued. Currently, in certain sports, there is an acceptance to utilize these resources to further the careers of the athlete.

I love what Matthew Henry's Concise Commentary says about 2 Timothy 2:5:

The great care of a Christian Believer (soldier) must be to please Christ. We are to strive to get the mastery of our lusts and corruptions, but we cannot expect the prize unless we observe the laws. We must take care that we do good in a right manner, that our good may not be spoken evil of. Some who are active, spend their zeal about outward forms and doubtful disputations. But those who strive lawfully shall be crowned at last. If we would partake the fruits, we must labor; if we would gain the prize, we must run the race. We must do the will of God, before we receive the promises, for which reason we have need of patience. Together with our prayers for others, that the Lord would give them understanding in all things, we must exhort and stir them up to consider what they hear or read.

CHAPTER (7)

The Husbandman

The husbandman that labors must be first partaker of the fruits. (2 Timothy 2:6)

Yeshua said these excellent words, "I am the true Vine and My Father is the Husbandman" (John 15:1). The Christ Believer is a branch connected to Yeshua, the Vine of God. The Husbandman, our Heavenly Father, will prune us so that we might bear fruit, and not be barren. We are also considered "trees of righteousness, the plantings of the Lord that bring Him glory" (Isaiah 61:3). And when we study the life of Yeshua, His utmost desire was to *do* the Will of the Father (Hebrews 10:7), thereby pleasing the Father as He was about the Father's business (Luke 2:49). This was His life, His true profession. He came to bring us the salvation of the Father. And for everything, every movement, He sought the council of the Father. And when He was in the ministry field, because of His prayer life that kept Him close to God, He could always hear the Father, obey Him, and the Father always heard Him (John 11:42). And seeing that there was nothing barren about Yeshua, I am encouraged that my Husbandman is making me a fruitful planting of the Lord because He prunes away the knowledge in us that is not like Him. In the book of 2 Peter

Chapter 1, it is filled with instructions on being fruitful in the knowledge of the Lord. Peter counsels that it is through the knowledge of God and Christ Yeshua that we receive grace and truth, glory, virtue, great and precious promises, the things we should diligently add to the Faith given to us that will lead us into a very fruitful life. Yes, and all that pertains to life and godliness so that we will lack nothing worthy of Him.

The husbandman is an intriguing term. The Oxford Reference describes this word as the old word for a farmer below the rank of "yeoman." And the yeoman referred to a man who owns and cultivates land, or a servant in a noble or royal household. His ranking could be between a sergeant and a groom or a squire and a page. In the Old Testament husbandman comes from the Hebrew Word 'adamah,' which means "land" or "of the earth." It is the same Hebrew word from which we get Adam, the name of the first man whom God made. This word also means, Husbandry, which is an agricultural term related to the production of crops or livestock. Additionally, husbandman meant a householder or master of the house. But now in our modern language it has been limited to farmer or tiller of the soil. Thus, to 'husband' is to manage something well, showing prudence and economic sense. Furthermore, husbandry is a term for a vineyard.

The main reason for tillage of the earth or soil is to make the soil loose and aerated (introduce air into) so that the roots of the plants may grow to proper depth. Too much tillage can incur damage.

"Dirt Connections" article gives us some pros and cons of tilling soil. They include:

Pros of Tilling soil:

1. Aerates the soil
2. Can help eliminate pests (like soil-borne larvae and insects that emerge in the spring
3. Can warm the soil in the Spring

4. Can help control weeds
5. Provides an opportunity to amend soil in the Fall
Cons of Tilling Soil:
 1. Can create 'hardpan' (a thick, dense layer of compacted soil that restricts the flow of nutrients and water through the soil due to over-tilling.)
 2. Can strip Nitrogen from the soil
 3. May promote erosion
 4. Can dry out the soil
 5. Time and energy of tilling can be a problem for those with back or other physical issues.

Philippians 2:13 tells us that it is God who works in us both to will and to do of His good pleasure. (I realize I say this often) He works in us as we seek Him, to understand His will, as we seek Him in repentance, fellowship, prayer for ourselves and others. He is the Husbandman who tills the soil of our earth/heart to make it soft, pliable and able to receive the seed of His word. However, the Father knows how often to till and how to preserve what He has already placed in us that we might have optimum growth and keep the best nourishment. Furthermore, look at what Hosea 10:12 tells us:

Sow to yourselves in righteousness, reap in mercy; break up your fallow ground: for it is time to seek the lord, till He come and rain righteousness upon you. The word 'fallow' refers to land which is untilled and uncultivated. This is ground which no plow has turned up and into which no seed is cast. It is possible that it was left to rest, that it may not exhaust itself, and that its internal resources may be all the richer afterwards. But as in the case of the words given by Hosea, the ground may have become encumbered with "thorns." Thus, in the scripture above, we can see that the breaking up of *our* fallow ground (hardheadedness, hardheartedness, stiff-neckedness, etc.) is accomplished by the instrument of prayer. Furthermore, the Christ Believer's prayerfulness or lack of can determine what type of 'ground' we have or can have. In the Gospel of Matthew (it is also found in the Gospels of Mark and Luke), there is a parable about the Sower. Yeshua talked to His disciples about the four (4) types of grounds by the which the precious seed can fall into:

1. Wayside Ground: This is where a person hears God's word, but does not understand, then comes the wicked to steal it from their heart before they can take root. It is like sowing the seed on a blacktop road. That kind of road which has no earth to receive it, cannot produce. The birds will surely come to get it.

2. Stony Ground: This is where the word of God was received with joy, but it doesn't have deep root in them. This person stays for a while, but when trials and persecutions come, they fall away because of offense.

3. Thorny Ground: This is where the person receives the word in the mix of dealing with many cares of life and desires. These things are like thorns that choke the life of the word from them and won't allow the word to be profitable for their soul.

4. Good Ground: This is where prayer is constant, and the heart has been cleansed and stays free of the distractions and the debris of carnal desires, unbelief, thorns and briers. The person is free to hear the word, understands it, and will bear fruit in various degrees.

Because the Husbandman is the one who works and prunes the vineyard, he is the one who is the first partaker of the fruits to discern whether or not he has a good crop. Therefore, as followers of Christ we are considered the first-fruits of God because of the redemptive work of Christ. And since God is our Husbandman and works diligently in us, at some point He will come looking for good fruit in us.

CHAPTER (8)

The Proving of the Soldier

Bertist Rouse wrote a book called, "The Little Foxes: Things Christians Do Not Have To Do." In one of his chapters (page 21) he ministered that the Christ Believer does not have to prove themselves. What he referred to was that the Believer does not have to always prove they are right. He/she doesn't have to wage war and get into trouble with anyone just to prove a point because the truth will eventually prevail. Most of us know that *standing down* is not always easy. You may be falsely accused, but to get into open battles that will hurt each other, damage our witness or damage an onlooker's chance of experiencing the grace and salvation of the Lord simply isn't worth it. We are accountable and responsible.

Also, Victor Yap wrote an article in which he titled, "Everything to Prove." This is what he said:

"None of us like the pressure of meeting others' expectations, fulfilling our potential, and showing one's worth. Even the previous year's NBA champions have to prove they were worthy champions, no fluke, and not a flash in the pan. Champions have to prove they were not lucky and also-rans (a loser in a race or other contest, especially by a large margin) have to prove they are not losers. Teachers and students have to prove themselves.

Professionals have to prove they know what they are doing. Voters need proof of residency and identity, drivers their proof of insurance, and customers their proof of purchase. Scientists have to prove their findings, mathematicians their calculation, chemist their formula, archaeologist their discovery, prosecutors their evidence, athletes their fitness, producers their ratings, and CEOs their salary. Laggards, rookies and veterans have something to prove, and young and old have something to prove. Sooner or later and to a greater or lesser degree, everyone has something to prove to oneself, if not to others."

I worked at a company where I held a very challenging position. I dealt with numbers all day long; fulfilling orders via emails, calls and faxes. There was a lot of pressure with the job and though there was ample training, there were a few times I wondered if I could really do it. Eyes were on me and I would sit, work and pray. Sometimes I was 'snowed under' with the work and I graciously received the help offered. But after a while on the job, I would not always immediately accept or even call for assistance because I knew I had to learn my position and prove to myself that I could do it. When I finally got the hang of it, I truly felt grateful, accomplished by grace and proven as an associate.

Desmond Doss' true story was featured in a movie called, "Hacksaw Ridge." According to the story, Desmond grew up in a dysfunctional family. Alcoholism and physical and domestic abuse plagued them through their father's struggle with PTSD and guilt because of being the only one in his military team that survived the war. Desmond's mother was a stabilizer in the family, being a woman of faith and prayer. However, Desmond and his brother fought continuously. One day, they got into a tussle again. Desmond, in his anger gave his brother a near fatal blow, hitting him on the head with a brick. From this event, Desmond sank into grief and remorse. Thankfully, his brother survived the blow, but Desmond turned to God repenting and seeking for forgiveness. He then made a vow to never use any weapon to hurt another person. When WWII broke out, Desmond wanted to serve his country by being a trained field Medic. The Military required him to learn how use a weapon. When he refused to abide by that particular requirement, he explained that his Faith came with the conviction to not use a weapon to harm people, but to use his skills to save them and minister life and healing to their wounds. This brought about much anger and persecution towards him from his fellow soldiers and the upper ranks. They could not conceive having a soldier that did not know how to use the weapons required as a soldier. Thus, they decided to do everything to make him quit. Additionally, Desmond took every verbal abuse and physical blow they could measure out to him. He tolerated every word of 'cowardice' they could run him down with. Finally, they took him to court as their last resort to kick him out of the military. God came to his rescue and gave him deliverance by using his father, a veteran to make a plea for him. Desmond won the case, but he was still looked on as a coward and unfit for the military and war.

Well, the time finally came for them to go to combat. Many of their men were killed, and quite a few were wounded. On that field of war, Desmond went from man to man helping those he could help, as well as rescuing those he could that were wounded from the crossfire and letting them down by ropes down the steep ridge to safety. When the battle got very heavy they had to retreat and regroup. But Desmond secretly stayed behind. He felt there were still wounded, yet alive soldiers there. And he did not want to leave any of his fellow soldiers on that ridge for the enemy troops to pick off. So, he *stealthily* rescued one man after another, then let each one of them down the steep ridge to the safety of his fellow guarding troops below.

At first, Desmond's military group didn't know who was bringing down their wounded men (even some wounded enemy soldiers), but word got out that it was Desmond who saved them from certain death if they had not been removed from that place. Desmond had no gun. No knife. No grenade. No nothing...but his Bible, prayer, his faith and his Medic bag. He trusted God to save him and the wounded men he went *praying* to get off the enemy territory.

When Desmond finally came down from the ridge, they all looked at him like he was some kind of ghost. Some were greatly ashamed at how they abused and maltreated him. While others changed their minds forever about him as a man. He became a hero and a man of God in their eyes. When it was time to back into combat, the troops did not want to go back up on that ridge unless Desmond first prayed for them and went up with them. *This made me cry!*

Desmond's faith had been placed on the 'proving (testing) ground.' It had to be proved that the God he confessed to know was able to save him without the required guns and other weapons of war. Desmond proved that he was not a coward, he proved that it was possible to be an excellent soldier and Medic and not carry a gun. He proved that the Lord was with him, and he proved his bravery and faithfulness to our country.

Moreover, there is a proving ground for every Believer at this present season. In whatever way the proving ground might reveal itself, we must prove that Christ lives in us by our walk of faith which produces righteousness. 2 Corinthians 13:5 (kjv) puts it like this, *"Examine yourselves, whether ye be in the faith; prove your own selves. Know ye not your own selves, how that Jesus Christ is in you, except ye be reprobates?"* The word 'examine' comes from the Greek word *peirazo*, which means to "scrutinize and try." A stronger word for examine in the Greek is *dokimazo*, which means to test as to metals. And the word reprobates is another word for unprofitable. A way to know if you are in the faith is that righteousness comes out of you in the heat of the moment, in trials or the hard times.

I also thought interesting what Joshua Infantado said about how we examine ourselves. He asked a serious question, "Other than your reflection, what do you see when you look in the mirror?" What do we look for, what do we need to fix, and ensure we are presentable? There is also a spiritual mirror that will help us examine ourselves. Mr. Infantado gave three ways on how we can examine ourselves:

1. Examine your faith—we are not beyond getting deceived. We don't blindly believe, we study what we receive (and turn it over with prayer asking the Lord to remove the veils from the scriptures that we might understand. He will give increase—Apostle Cornelius Perry).
2. Examine your works—(we allow for the works of righteousness to manifest out of us and we ask to receive the spirit of the Law—Apostle C. Perry).
3. Examine yourself through the perspective of God— we allow the Lord to show us His heart in every situation.

We have discussed that when the soldier enlists into a branch of service, they have to go through a series of training. They cannot pass on from the basics until they prove they can do what is required according to the standard of that branch of service. The Christ Believer goes through series of tests as well. It may be in the area of integrity, relationships, workplace, or the home life. Until we learn to receive the grace of God to deal righteously in all areas, we may find ourselves having to continue to go through some of the same things until we can prove ourselves in those areas.

CHAPTER (9)

The Good Soldier Learns and Moves in Conscience

Less than two months after moving to North Carolina in 2016 and hearing the powerful ministry of New Jerusalem Church, one morning while praying in my bedroom, an individual came to my thoughts. This made me very uncomfortable because I had hurt this person and I knew the Lord was dealing with me to find and reach out to them. It was a difficult situation to face, but when we finally connected, I confessed some hard things about what I'd done. To my surprise and joy, they told me they had forgiven me a long time ago and that Jesus had forgiven me too. I solemnly thank the Lord!

After that conversation, I examined myself as to why it was so difficult to admit my sin and error. The things I said were true, but I still didn't want to believe that about me. I wanted to think that I was better than that. But I wasn't. Furthermore, as I heard the Truth about the Old Nature (also called the Old Man) we were born into this world with, alongside peering into the Mirror of God's Word, the scales of my life did not balance: I was lacking. It took some time for me to truly believe that that evil nature will ALWAYS be found lacking. It has flaws that can NEVER be changed. Though it can do some good, there is always evil in the 'mix'; yes, even in its good. Since that epic moment in time, the Almighty has been peeling back layers of the 'veils' of my life so that I can *see* me, comprehend why He had to come and save us, and fathom why He said, "You must be born again." (John 3:3) Hence, my first real introduction to "The Purged Conscience" was at New Jerusalem Church in Wendell, North Carolina.

Prior to my move to NC, I had made a deliberate geographical move to Kansas in May of 2015. I had recently graduated with a Bachelor's of Science and it was my full intention to stay in Kansas and move forward with my life doing the thing I really enjoyed and loved...singing. At the time, I was staying with a missionary couple, Steve and Deb (Steve has passed on to his heavenly home- (April 2022).

At the end of that same month on Saturday, May 30, 2015 (Memorial Day), I had a beautiful experience with the Lord. I was given a clean slate in life and a brand new Path. About a week later in church, this experience was established as truth by the pastor of the church Steve and Deb attended...I did not know that man. Through a Word of Knowledge the pastor expressed almost exactly what the Lord had spoken in private inwardly to me. This was so exciting, yet, I did not understand the necessity or the depth of the renewing of my mind that was needed at that time. Or the fact that my clean slate also meant I was placed on the road to recovery—at its beginning.

Another thing I will add, during that first month of my stay in Kansas, I received a surprise call from my cousin, Delorris (Dee), who lived in North Carolina. She invited me to her church's Women's Conference—all expenses paid. *I flat refused the invitation!* She was undaunted by my refusal because she called me the very next evening and brought up the subject again. I was still uninterested, but this time I did not flat refuse. It seemed that I should listen more to what she was saying. She then asked me to strongly consider the event, pray about going and she would call me back in a week. Needless to say, I found myself in North Carolina that July 2015.

When I arrived at the Women's Conference, things started moving and shaking in my life. By that time, I had only been in Kansas for two months. But I felt an alarming need to move again... to North Carolina, and come under the tutelage of the ministry of New Jerusalem Church. Though I felt it was the right move to make, it frustrated me. There was an internal struggle with this tentative move that was terribly unsettling because I had just moved to the state of Kansas. I wanted to fulfill the dream in my heart and I knew this would mean another delay. Furthermore, I did not have the means for another move. So, I told the Lord that if this is His Will, provide, and I will make the move to North Carolina. Well, as the story goes, "Kansas was history". And my plans were rerouted and I ended up in North Carolina only 9 1/2 months after moving to Kansas.

Going back to that trip and my first week in North Carolina, that experience at NJC's Women's Conference was life-changing. It made me see a severity of my brokenness inside and I knew I had to move there and hear the ministry if my life was going to truly be healthy. I was dealing with the residue of not only a broken heart, but a shattered life—though I had been given a clean slate and a brand-new Path. Yet still...my life began anew.

During the 3 1/2 years I lived in North Carolina, I learned much concerning what had happened to me and why. And I was brought to the realization of facing the "me" that had brought me so many troubles. Another powerful, yet gradual event that took place while in North Carolina is that through the continual teaching of the Gospel of Jesus and the demonstration of love, the Lord broke down my paper-thin resistance and persuaded me that He *deeply* and eternally loved me and could forgive me, restore me and heal my wounds, brokenness, and make me a new vessel that did not bear the signs of 'damaged goods'.

Many of us have seen a military individual return home with certain physical injuries: burn wounds, missing arms, legs, feet, face, ears, etc. In other instances, the wounded soldier may have, coupled with their physical wounds a condition called, Post Traumatic Stress Disorder, or (PTSD). It can go on for years with the soldier reliving the traumas with flashbacks, nightmares of the events, guilt, anger, growling fits of rage, and hallucinations, of the agonizing things they experienced on the fields of war.

Our war vets are not the only ones who can develop PTSD, many civilians in our country suffer from it as well.

An article called the, "National Institute of Mental Health (NIMH)" reveals risk factors of persons of every age. Some of these include:

Living through dangerous events and traumas

Getting hurt or seriously injured

Childhood traumatic

Feeling horror, helplessness, or extreme fear

Having little or no social support after the event has taken place

Dealing with extra stress after the event, such as the death of a loved one, pain and injury, or loss of a job or home

Having a history of mental illness or substance abuse.

When we meet wounded people, they are not always easy to detect. But in some of these cases, the wounded have suffered through numerous afflictions. Some things are *unspeakable,* giving some individuals a very hard exterior, *or* making some people meaner than a junk yard dog, or so terribly introverted they have difficulty meeting people, or just hard to get along with. Some will do anything to mask their hurt, fears, and insecurities with a smile. For some, the wounds come from a messy divorce, death, tragedy; and sometimes the tragedies are manifest from their own error or sin. Furthermore, some are bankrupt, broken, and homeless. These 'wounded souls' are at the mercy of either kindness or cruelty. We have a choice as to how we are going to respond to them.

In the New Testament a beggar named Lazarus' lived a life that is one type, slant, or description of the wounded. Lazarus was daily _laid_ at the gate of a rich man's home. This reveals that Lazarus was not able to take care of himself properly (Luke 16:19-31). The rich man was very well off. The scriptures say the rich man was clothed in purple and fine linen and fared sumptuously or lavishly _every_ day. Lazarus' situation was a helpless one. He had to be laid at that gate to beg for even the crumbs. This can be a very humiliating thing for a person who begs just to have a little something to eat. Though the rich man _did_ see Lazarus, he refused to give him anything. Lazarus was full of sores and received more comfort from the dogs that came and licked his sores (Luke 16:21). Sadly, there was no compassion in the rich man's heart for Lazarus, even though he could have helped him without feeling any loss.

Being at the bottom does not feel good. Your contribution seems too small or never enough. When a wounded person feels that way, it is very easy for them to try to do what is not yet in their power or means to do to compensate for their lack. They may be overly helpful, which could in turn, open a door for abuse. The one who has the advantage can look at that person and know, "Wow, that could have been me!" and deal with them tenderly. On the other side of the coin, the person can become a victim, and receive deeper wounds by falling into the hands of someone who sees them as a stepping stone for selfish gain. There are so many stories in the past and present to give as examples of the atrocities of injured lives. Sometimes it takes a little patience, gentleness and kindness in the loving introduction of our Savior to them and they can be healed. This has very much to do with which conscience we operate in. And as soldiers of Christ, our purged conscience must rule over us. But we have to daily exercise ourselves in it.

Once a person is enlisted into a military branch of service, that soldier is *conditioned* to groom him/herself with particular care. They are taught various things, as Mr. Johnson confirms: how they make their beds, shine their shoes or boots, the cleanliness of their bodies and crispness of their clothes, how they walk, talk, and how they honor rank or authority. In case of impending war, they have been trained on the ground, with repetitive physical and mental exercises that are, at times, gruesome. Some of these men and women come into peak fitness and powerful physiques. I have seen military persons who were older, but they still carried themselves in a way that spoke loudly of their training as a soldier.

There is a conditioning that comes with the Kingdom life. It involves the renewing of our minds. It involves allowing the Christ Mind to reign in us through consciousness. As we continue to follow the Lord, we begin to think like our Creator; responding righteously to difficult people and situations of life, speak like him, hear His instructions and obey (John 5:19). We become conditioned to live out of a conscience that won't let us live the way they were naturally born, but rather, like the Lord, who redeemed us, gave us a new birth and translated us out of the Kingdom of darkness into His Kingdom (Colossians 1:13).

Another aspect of training is the soldier's weapons of war such as, strategic negotiating, stealth training, knives, grenades, sticky bombs, missiles or rocket/torpedoes, and how to be sharpshooters or archers. They are trained in watchfulness, how to read their surroundings, as well as reading their fellow soldier. They have to have a tight reign over themselves in order to stay alert and vigilant.

As a soldier of the Lord, the Believer, must learn to know and understand him/herself and what is going on _inside_ of them at all times, having learned to exercise their purged conscience in the process of daily living and keeping their emotions washed with the water of the Word. This exercising is like intense prayer, and will allow the follower of Christ to reckon dead the old nature and old way of life and will keep the them from many, many evils because they will come to know that they live because of Christ who lives in them, having died to their own self.

Within the pure conscience is the ability or power to maintain the commitment made to be a soldier and not go AWOL (absent without official leave). As stated earlier, prayer is the key here; a mighty weapon of war for the Believer. Prayer is what enables us to access the grace of God. It is desperately needed in the hardest of times and is key to how we remain faithful to the Lord, steadfast and immovable in our dedication, love and commitment to Him. If we learn how to use this weapon, we will be able to witness as well as say what it is written in Acts 24:16:

"And herein do I exercise myself to have always a conscience void of offense against God and man" (Acts 24:16).

CHAPTER (10)

The Soldier's Covenant

The term "Covenant" has grown to be something endearing to me because in my experience over the last seven years, it represents eternal love, and grew to mean a sense of belonging or belonging to S*omeone*.

The Hebrew word for covenant is 'Berit, Berith or Beriyth'. It is derived from the Hebrew word, 'Barah' which means "to cut." It also means, "to bind." It is more than a contract between two parties. It is a pact, an alliance or treaty. It refers to the relationship between God and His people, Israel. And now to the Christ-Believer. It is synonymous with God's law, the Decalogue. And in the Decalogue, the word 'berith' is used as an idiom for "covenant".

Covenants had weight as we look at Old Testament examples. However, as sin increased in the earth, the power of its ties seemed to deteriorate, not because the Lord God is unfaithful, not because it was outdated, but because humanity constantly sought out its own ways when the going got tough (me included). Thus, we live in a society— and it's spreading across cultures and continents where covenants no longer have binding power. The author of Romans understood this when he said:

"Without understanding, covenant-breakers, without

natural affection, implacable, unmerciful" (Romans 1:31).

The books of Ephesians and Hebrews gives us beautiful understanding of the covenant the Believer has been brought into through the death, burial and resurrection of Yeshua Christ. We will look briefly into this wonderful covenant in just a little bit.

The term "Oath" bears a *kinsman* meaning to what we call covenant. However, there is a difference. Also, an oath can be said to precede or confirm a covenant. When a man or woman enters a branch of service, they are sworn in. There is an enlistment oath that the Armed Forces must make to serve our country and be true to the governing laws over them as enlistees. Here is an example of that oath:

(a) Enlistment Oath.—Each person enlisting in an armed force shall take the following oath:

"I, _____, do solemnly swear (or affirm) that I will support and defend the Constitution of the United States against all enemies, foreign and domestic; that I will bear true faith and allegiance to the same; and that I will obey the orders of the President of the United States and the orders of the officers appointed over me, according to regulations and the Uniform Code of Military Justice. So help me God."

(b) Who May Administer.—The oath may be taken before the President, the Vice-President, the Secretary of Defense, any commissioned officer, or any other person designated under regulations prescribed by the Secretary of Defense.

Though this avowal is similar to a covenant, it is not perpetual, it is in force as long as the enlistee serves as a part of this branch of service. However, if the oath is broken, it could mean a dishonorable discharge.

Despite the fact one of the definitions of the covenant

affirms itself as a contract, nevertheless, there is also a difference between a contract and a covenant. An article by "Up-council" has given us some clarity on the differences between these two important agreements:

Contracts are agreements enforceable by law. Here are some components to a valid agreement:

It must have an offer and the offer accepted

It must have valuable consideration. This means the parties are exchanging something that is equally valuable to the other.

Both parties must have the legal and mental capacity to enter into a contract.

One party cannot force the other party to sign a contract.

The consideration offer is legal.

Covenants are written promises between two or more parties where the party either pledges to do something (called an affirmative covenant) or refrains from doing something (called a negative covenant). It is a type of contract. In a covenant, the person making the promise is the covenantor, and the person who is benefiting from the promise is a coventee.

Let's look at some contrasting facts:

While a contract is legally binding, a covenant is a spiritual agreement.

A contract is an agreement between parties while a covenant is a spiritual pledge.

A contract is an agreement you can break while a covenant is a perpetual promise. And while you sign a contract, you seal a covenant.

The scriptures give us several examples of covenants made by God. Here are a few:

Adamic Covenant: This covenant was between God, His Man and His Woman. They were given dominion over the fish of the sea, and over the fowl of the air, and over the cattle, and over all the earth, and over every creeping thing that creeps upon the earth. They were blessed so they could be fruitful, and multiply, replenish the earth, and to subdue it and have dominion over it. (Genesis 1:26-28). Before God took the woman out of Adam, He gave Adam this command, saying, "Of every tree of the Garden, you may freely eat; but the tree of the knowledge of good and evil, you shall not eat of it: for in the day you eat of it, you shall surely die" (Genesis 2: 16-17).

Noahic Covenant: Deals with Noah and his sons, their seed after them, every living Creature out of the Ark, and the Earth. In this covenant, the Lord God promised to never destroy all flesh or the earth with the waters of a flood. He even put His 'bow' (rainbow) in the sky as a reminder of this (Genesis 9:8-17). Most of us have seen a rainbow; one of the beautiful wonders of the world. And to think, just its presence represents a binding covenant/promise God made to mankind.

Abrahamic Covenant: Abraham's covenant started with a promise from God to have an heir from his own body. He was old. The land of Canaan was assigned to Abraham to possess. Abraham was told by God that his offspring would be strangers in a foreign land. They would eventually be enslaved and oppressed for four hundred years and the Lord would finally execute judgment on those who tyrannized them. God then gave Abraham the map of the land assigned to him and his offspring (Genesis 15: 1-21). Abraham was given the covenant of circumcision (Genesis 17:1-14). Every male had to be circumcised in the foreskin of his genitals. Abraham's immediate obedience (Genesis 17:23) to the Lord revealed his faith in God.

Mosaic Covenant: This is basically called the Old Covenant or the Law of Moses. The provisions contained in the 613 commandments were the blessings for obedience and the curses for disobedience. God cut this conditional covenant with Israel at Mount Sinai (Exodus 19-24). This was rehearsed to them in Deuteronomy Chapter 11.

Covenant made at Moab: This covenant is likened unto a 'second law.' Israel was preparing to enter the Promised Land. Moses was there to help them reaffirm and continue the covenant that was enacted at Mt Sinai/Horeb almost 40 years prior. There, at the plains of Moab, Israel was led to renew their commitment to keep the Laws and be a nation that was true to their God (Deuteronomy 30).

Davidic Covenant: God gave David an unconditional covenant that included these things: (1). Making David's name great. (2). God Himself will provide and plant His people Israel in a place where they will not be harmed or disturbed. (3). The Lord will establish a house for David and establish David's kingdom through his offspring. David's offspring (Solomon and eventually Jesus) will build a house for the Lord and God will establish that man's throne forever. And God will never take His love from that man. (4). Thus, David's house and kingdom will endure forever before the Lord. And David's throne will be established forever (2 Samuel 7:8-16, 2 Samuel 23:5, Luke 1: 32-33, Mark 10:77).

The New Testament Covenant: The Law of Moses was a school master. It was necessary because it led us to Christ (Galatians 3:24). The people who were under the Law could not keep it the because they did not have a conscience that could witness their cleansing (Hebrews 10:1-2). The New Covenant brings us into a conscience that is pure because it has been purged by the very Blood of Christ (Hebrews 9:14). This beautiful covenant connected with (Jeremiah 31:31-34) and is a Covenant that allows the conscience to witness what Christ did when He put the Old Nature to death. God writes the pact of this awesome covenant in our hearts and in our minds (Hebrews 10:16). And as we seek God in prayer concerning our covenant, He strengthens us to walk it out and reckon our own selves dead to the former nature. It is also found in (Hebrews 8-9. Matthew 26:28, Hebrews 8:6-13, Hebrews 9:15).

The New Covenant deals with the spirit of one very active Entity in the Believer through consciousness, manifested in two ways: (1) *"To love the Lord our God with all our hearts, souls, minds, and strength. (2) And to love our neighbor as ourselves. On these two directives hang all the Law and the Prophets"* (Matthew 22:34-40). Love is the Spirit of the Law. Love is the fulfillment of the Law. When we love, we won't offend. When we love, we won't put an idol before the one true God, Yah, Yahweh. When we love, we won't take His name in vain, or intentionally hurt someone, murder, commit adultery, steal, or covet (lust) the belongings or spouses, or homes, cars of others. When we learn to walk in love, thinking evil and speaking evil will die in us and becomes a thing of the past. This takes learning to walk in our new nature and the power of the Spirit of God.

When I look at the Book of Ephesians, Chapter 2, I greatly rejoice because some of the benefits are spelled out. For instance: The New Testament covenant is a covenant of grace. And we have been given the Spirit of God who guides us into all truth (John 16:13). The faith of God is in our conscience and our hearts. And as we seek Him, asking the help of His Spirit, we have the capability to grow up in Him and manifest the kind of 'Light beings' He originally made us.

We were born into this world dead in our trespasses and sins (Ephesians 2:1,5). But when the Good News of Christ Yeshua is preached, faith is aroused and confronts us. As we continue to hear the Gospel and what the Lord did, faith comes into our heart and we become more conscious of our sinfulness. Thus, conviction of sin is awakened. When conviction is embraced, we will soon come to repent of our sin, acknowledging our need for the Savior. And in the midst of the throes of true repentance, the Lord forgives us and quickens us from the dead. We are born again and then brought into the covenant of our Lord Yeshua. He makes us 'light and salt' in Him (Matthew 5:13-16). And we become God's workmanship or masterpiece created in Christ Yeshua unto good works. At that point we are 'babes' and drink the sincere milk of God's word. We must learn to pray to the one who feeds us and takes care of us.

Our precious leaders in the church plant and water, but God gives the increase (1 Corinthians 3:6-7) that allows us to receive and absorb the nourishment (life, Spirit and power) of God's word. We have been given access to the very throne of God through Christ's death, burial and resurrection, so when we cry out, He comes. When we have incidents, He helps us. When we fall down trying to walk, He picks us up and helps us to our feet so our legs can grow strong to walk. As a good Parent, the Lord will aid and guide us in what is right. Moreover, as stated earlier, we are citizens of heaven. In our growth, we are being made and brought into the fullness of who we already are in Him, and He through the preaching of the word, lays His foundation in us.

CHAPTER (11)

The Dedicated/The Committed

I remember the first time I read the story about Achan. It was not an easy read. But let me just lay a groundwork to lead up to this story. I will start with where Moses, the leader of God's people, Israel, had already died, and Joshua was placed by election of God over Israel as Moses' successor. After over 40 years of wandering in the desert, they finally came to the entrance of the land God had told them about.

The Lord did several things to prepare them to enter the land of promise. First, the Lord encouraged Joshua; He promised Joshua that He would not fail him and would be with him as He was with Moses. He told Joshua to be strong and very courageous because everything that would be asked of him he would be able to do. Also, as a major preempt for good success, He encouraged Joshua to absorb the book of the Law. It was not to depart from Joshua's mouth, but he was to meditate in it day and night (Joshua 1). This was crucial. And in this observance, Joshua and the people could be invincible to their enemies. Secondly, Joshua's officers were commanded to pass throughout the camp in proclamations that in three days the people were to prepare to cross the Jordan into the land of promise, whereby they would begin to take possession of the land.

After the people heard those words, they all agreed to be obedient to the Lord. Thirdly, Joshua sent out two spies to view the land and gain information of its layout. They lodged in the house of Rahab, a harlot who lived on the great wall of the city of Jericho. When the spies' whereabouts were discovered, Rahab hid the spies on her roof under some flax. When she was questioned by the authorities concerning them, she did tell them that they had come to her home, but they has already escaped, fleeing to the mountains.

Rahab, and all of Jericho and the surrounding nations had heard about the miracles of the Lord, and what He had done to Egypt and the two kings of the Amorites. She also knew that Jericho was 'going down,' and she was terrified. She showed honor to the God of Israel by acknowledging His greatness as the One true God. And because she saved the Israelite spies from harm, she pleaded with them for the salvation of their God for herself and her family. Seeing she had done this thing for them, a conditional pact was struck between them for her and her family to be saved from the coming devastation of Jericho...that is, if she would not reveal the business of their visit and also if she would hang out a scarlet cord from her window (Joshua 2).

After this, came the miraculous event of the parting of the Jordan River, and Israel crossed over the Jordan on dry ground, which was similar to when Israel crossed the Red Sea or Sea of Reeds (Exodus 14). After they crossed the Jordan, the Lord commanded Joshua to circumcise the children of Israel (males) the *second time* (Joshua 5:2-3). This instruction was paramount because those who left Egypt were circumcised, but almost all of them died in the wilderness and a new uncircumcised generation of Israel was born in the wilderness and had to be brought into the Covenant of Circumcision (Joshua 5:2-9).

Now Israel's first military assignment after crossing the Jordan was the city of Jericho. The name Jericho is Arabic and means, "Place of Fragrance or City of the Moon." Jericho was a great walled and fortified city. During that time, Jericho was about five acres in size. Jericho is commonly known as the oldest city in the world. And is an important, historical, and political center located northwest of the Dead Sea There has been stories that the top of the walls of Jericho were so thick and wide (twenty feet wide) that chariots could be driven on them.

Well, the time came for Israel to make their first military attack in the land of promise. The king of Jericho put the city on strict watch and placed their own city under siege, allowing no one to come in or go out because they knew that the God of Israel and His people were coming.

Again, the Lord encouraged Joshua by telling him, *"See, I have given into your hand Jericho and the king thereof and the mighty men of valor."* He then gave Joshua specific instructions:

1. Joshua and the men of war were instructed to march around the city once. This was to be done for six days, with seven priests carrying trumpets made from ram's horns.

2. The Ark of the Covenant followed the priests.

3. On the seventh day, they were to march around the city seven times, while the priests blow the trumpets.

4. When they sounded the long blast with the ram's horns, the entire Israeli army were instructed to cry out loud.

5. At this point, the wall would collapse and the soldiers were instructed to charge into the city of Jericho.

6. Mind you, the Lord had given another most daunting instruction: the city was pronounced by the Lord as accursed or devoted for destruction. NOTHING was to be taken as spoil. No captives. The Lord did instruct them that the silver, gold, and vessels of brass and iron would be consecrated to the Lord and placed in His treasury. But they were not to take anything for themselves; only Rahab and her family would be kept alive if she and her family

followed the instruction of the spies. They were further informed that if they disobeyed and took anything from out of Jericho for themselves, they would also become accursed and come under the same ban of destruction (Joshua 6:17-19). Everything the Lord God told them came to pass. And God gave them the victory over Jericho.

The next military assignment was to a small place called "Ai." Because Joshua and the leaders with him did not acknowledge the Lord about the military strategy for this place, but sent only a few men of war to the conflict, they lost the battle and some of their men. Joshua was devastated. He fell to his face in grief seeking the Lord. His faith was shaken. God told him to get up because *Israel* had sinned by taking things devoted for destruction. This is where the story gets to Achan. He and his family were of the tribe of Judah.

Well, they cast lots. And it fell on the tribe of Judah. Out of Judah, the lot fell on the family of Zarhites. After Zarhites, the lot fell on the family Zodi. Lastly, Achan, the son of Carmi. With the gentle prompting of Joshua, Achan finally confessed that he had sinned against the Lord. He lusted after and took a Babylonian garment that he had seen. He also took some silver and some gold and hid them in the earth inside of his tent. When they searched and found the articles Achan had stolen, Joshua and all Israel took Achan, his family, his animals, his tent and all he had to the valley of Achor. There, they were all stoned and burned with fire (Joshua 7). This was a very sad event, most unfortunate; one person's sin affected the whole Israelite nation and lives were lost—including Achan and his family. Even now, when we sin against the Lord, others are greatly affected, harmed, soiled or jaded by the evil we do.

If anyone despised or rejected Moses' Law, they died without mercy on the basis of two or three witnesses (Hebrews 10:29). In this case, Achan and his whole family died because of his rebellion and disobedience.

I am so grateful for our Covenant! However, I have wondered severally, what could have happened if Achan had immediately confessed and repented? Would it have changed the outcome of his life and family? And what about the lives of the men who were slain in the battle of Ai?

Another thought could be shared here; Joshua was a great leader to Israel, however, as stated earlier, on this occasion he did not seek the council of the Lord. There was also another time when Joshua failed to seek the council of the Lord and again, things went wrong. That time it had to do with the Gibeonites in Joshua 9. These Gibeonites were a part of the territory that Israel was commissioned to conquer and possess. However, when these people came to Israel, they came in deception; as people from a far country, though they did not dwell far from the city of Ai. They were afraid for their lives so they came as impostors and drew Joshua into a covenant with them. Because Joshua and the leaders did not pray and seek the Face and approval of the Lord about these people, they were stuck with their decision. This became a snare to them. But they had to keep the pact they made with Gibeon.

Most, if not all followers of Christ can relate to this. We forget, because we are so accustomed to just doing what we want until the task is too big for us. Then we remember to seek the council of the Lord. But how can we fail when we acknowledge the Lord in all our ways? He promises to direct our path (Proverbs 3:5-6).

As mentioned earlier, the Law of Moses was a "school master" that leads us to Christ. It leads us to the New Testament where we see and experience the mercy of God in our transgressions and disobedience. We also receive forgiveness, and grace and truth to live for the Lord, the same God of the Old Testament.

Unless the Lord works in us, we simply cannot see

ourselves. We cannot see our unrighteousness, our greed, lust, and pride. Unless He reveals, we cannot see or understand the Almighty. But He is not willing that we perish. He has given us, who are a sinful people, a 'Door' that we can enter and be reconciled to Him, learn of Him, learn how to pray, and be transformed into His very image. That Door is none other than the Lord Yeshua. When the unregenerate and/or sinning Believer contritely cries out, seeking to find repentance, mercy, forgiveness and cleansing of sin, God, through the sacrifice of and advocacy of Christ, hears that person and forgives them. Truly, our prayer lives can make the difference between life and death simply because by acknowledging the Lord in all we do, He can keep us from great evils.

When I think about that word, 'devoted' in the context of these passages in Joshua, it seemed to reveal a dark side of devotion. But we know that there is a bright side that this word carries. And one of its synonyms, commitment, is a word we often hear in the House of God and our work places. Commitment, in relation to the Lord can be defined as devotion, dedication, or undivided loyalty to God.

I read some beautiful truths about commitment to God in an article by "Salt and Light Ministries." It revealed some of the things our pastor faithfully teaches us. This commitment to God is manifested as a *'Sold Out'* commitment. Not the kind of *selling out* that a person does when they have betrayed another and sold them out for unlawful gain, but the kind of selling out where the body, soul, mind and spirit is willingly given over to God and His desire and purpose. The scripture in Romans 12:1-2 reads like this:

> *1)I beseech you therefore, brethren, by the*
> *mercies of God, that ye present your bodies a*
> *living sacrifice, holy, acceptable unto God, which*
> *is your reasonable service.*

2)And be not conformed to this world: but be ye transformed by the renewing of your mind, that ye may prove what is that good, and acceptable, and perfect, will of God.

The Salt and Light article shared several things that represent our total commitment to God:

1. Being a living sacrifice means we have surrendered ourselves to the Lord. He is priority. And sometimes it means we give up that which is precious to us to put Him first.
2. To the depth we commit to God is the depth we are transformed. (Little commitment, little manifested transformation. Total commitment, total manifested transformation).
3. Submitting to His will, which is the highest and best way for us.
4. Exercising the gifts that God has placed in us according to His grace for the edifying and equipping of the saints.
5. Encouraging people, contributing to the work of God, His people, leading in righteousness, and showing mercy.
6. Hating evil: We increase in our love of righteousness and hatred of evil when we grow in genuine love and compassion for people whose lives have been destroyed by sin. Also, when we seek to experience a greater union and deeper relationship with our Lord God and Savior, who loves righteousness and hates wickedness.

In one of our services (1/18/2023), Apostle/Pastor Perry asked us this question: *"Do we know the commitment it takes to die for something?* Moreover, our total commitment yields to show forth the holiness of God (which is also revealed in moral purity, spiritual wholeness, separation from evil to a complete dedication to God) in everything, in all we do. It involves a lifestyle that brings honor to Christ in our words, thoughts and our actions.

CHAPTER (12)

Prayerlessness: The Silent Killer

Many years ago while driving to work one morning, the Lord began to impress on me reasons why I didn't see some things happening in my life and why as a Body of Believers we don't see His movements, healing, and miracles as a norm. It was because of the lack of seeking Him out in truth" and the lack of real 'worship'.

In one of our NJC services we were taught about the ten lepers (Luke 17:12-19). They all cried out for the Lord to have mercy on them and heal them of their death (leprosy). The Lord, who is very merciful, spoke the words of life. He simply told them to go and show themselves to the priests. As they went, they were ALL healed. But one of them, a Samaritan, when he saw that he was healed, came back to Yeshua and fell down worshiping Him. This man acknowledged his healing and gave thanks to God Most High. Please note again, ALL of them were healed, and the Lord did not take it back from them. The revelation here was that this one came knowing that his early death sentence was cut off and he would be able to have another chance to live again. His choice was to give back his whole life, his aspirations (which had been shattered) to the God who delivered him from such a horrific life. *By giving back to God the life restored to him, it would become a whole life worship unto God Most High.* The former leper was saying that all he was and all he intended to do and be, now belonged to the One who saved him. His life was God's...forever. *That is worship!*

Like those lepers, we come to the Lord in our desperation, and when He answers, for a moment we rejoice in Him and what He did, then, often times we go back to the same way we were, only to live a more raggedy life than before. God forgive me! Forgive us! What disdain we reveal is in our hearts towards the Lord! Most of us would not appreciate nor tolerate this type of treatment for too long. Yet we do this to the Lord consistently. It shows me that my prayer life is not a part-time job. It is my life profession. It is who I am in Christ. It is how I can draw close. It is how I am developed properly into His Woman. It is what I do because He is my life.

When I gaze at the life of Yeshua, the Captain of our salvation (Hebrews 2:10), the one thing I see Him doing a lot of, especially in the Gospel of Luke, is praying. (I desire to pattern my life after Him). Through His life of prayer, He developed a fellowship and union with the Father that is undeniable and unbreakable. The Book of Luke unveils to us that He often withdrew to the wilderness to pray (Luke 5). One of the critical fail-areas of the Believer is prayerlessness. For lack of proper usage of our weapon of prayer, many soldiers of God's Army have fallen prey to the devious ploys of the devil and their own flesh nature. This weapon of warfare can be used as a caution-device to keep us from falling headlong into the bowels of sin. If neglected, the Believer may unwittingly experience a depth of their sin-nature that is outside of their conscience that has been purged with the Blood of Christ. And some *type* of death is always connected with sin.

Prayer helps us stay connected to our pure conscience, which is the consciousness of God, and is the most powerful weapon in connection with God's word. Through prayer we stay on track with the Lord. Furthermore, the word of God is vital to us, and knowledge is power. But having the scriptures without going after the God of the scriptures leads us to an empty, powerless, heady, high-minded life, unable to have power over our own body, and void of right relationship with our Creator and His power. Yeshua, told the Sadducees that they were going wrong because they did not know the scriptures or the power of God (Matthew 22:1-29). And instead of honestly seeking the Father about who Yeshua really was, they were jealous and spent much more time seeking to find error in Him and could not see or accept that this Man was righteous and spoke the Truth.

Our frail humanity is no match for the god of this world and the darkness of his kingdom. But fervent prayer will usher us into the Throne Room of YAH. He is able to make us effective and consistent—if we will yield ourselves to Him. His authority and power in us will make us to stand firm in and on His foundation and resist evil. And the word of God will come to life in us.

Prayerlessness is no joke! As God's nation, our lukewarmness is at an alarming high! It speaks of a people who want what He has, but do not want *Him*. There are several things, (and more than what is mentioned here) that prayerlessness will breed in the Believer:

1. **Straying: Which brings separation between us and the Lord**

    a. There are several types of separation, some for righteous purpose, and some for evil purposes. In the separation that comes from prayerlessness, a coldness towards God begins to set in, and confusion as to why we don't feel the Presence of the Lord as before. Distressing thoughts can invade and bring an unsettling in the mind. And fear is able to torment in the slightest issues of life.

b. This is where carelessness begins...

2. A disregard for gathering together to hear the ministry of God's word:

a. Oh, how easy it is to put off being in the house of God! As a nation, we have come through several years of the pandemic. Many have had to find a way to make ends meet because of the layoffs. But it was necessary for as many as possible to be home. Some of our churches found means to get the word to us via Live Stream, Facebook and other methods. And as we became comfortable with being at home, we discovered the ease of just clicking on our computers or phones and we could hear the precious words of life from a 'sent' preacher. The Pandemic revealed something: it showed us our faithfulness or lack of to God and to the House of God. It was a time to hone in to the Lord and give ourselves more than we ever have. Some found that place with the Lord, while others drifted away. Prayerlessness will speak to us and will tell us we are alright and don't need to hear the word *that* often or be so 'churchy'. But the gathering to hear God's word is paramount. And many times, neglecting to gather to hear the word could cause us to miss our season of intimacy and elevation.

3. Fleshly desires move in:

a. When prayerlessness gets strong in us, the old nature is aroused from its death. Resisting the temptations of the body and thoughts goes from minuscule, all the way to very difficult. If the Believer will run to the Almighty at these critical intervals, they could be kept from making life-devouring mistakes.

4. Rebellion sets up in our hearts against the Lord:

a. This is or can be likened unto what the Lord said about Lucifer:

For you have said in your heart: 'I will ascend into heaven, I will exalt my throne above the stars of God; I will also sit on the mount of the congregation on the farthest sides of the north; I will ascend above the heights of the clouds, I will be like the Most High" (Isaiah 14:12-14).

Rebellion most always breeds disobedience. One way to describe this is that because the person has separated themselves from the Lord, they have dropped their connection with Him. When this happens the life of the word they have heard is being choked out. Lust has a doorway and gets a hold of them, and pulls them away from the safety of the Presence of the Lord, and then rebellion takes the individual and places them in a powerful prison. Here the heart becomes hardened. Their fellowship with the Lord is greatly distracted or there is none. Mostly, the Believer knows that they are erring, but little by little becomes powerless to come against it and in some cases, they do not even want the prayers of others who have been empowered to bring them out of it. In this prison, the Believer can be deceived and think it is their freedom to do what they want to do and whatever pleases them, yet going into a deeper hole of deception. Sometimes reckless movements are made and the individual has become blind and insensitive to the hurt they are incurring on themselves and others. The object before them is what they want and no one, not even God will stop them. The blindness of the Believer, (which the god of this world inflicts) covers them, and is often lifted *after* they have done great harm. Then they will be able to see the err of their way. That which follows is the horrible, tormenting guilt and shame that has already been described earlier. The enemy of our soul enjoys removing his blindfold when he thinks the Believer has gone too far out of the Lord's reach.

5. **Disobedience concerning the things we know to do.**

   a. Samson was one of the judges of Israel. He was unique in the Vision of God. His example is spectacular and heart-breaking at the same time. Before he was born, and in his mother's womb, he was called a Nazirite (or Nazarite). The Nazirite, (from the Hebrew nazar, means "to abstain from: or to consecrate oneself to"), among the ancient Hebrews, a sacred person whose separation was most commonly distinguished by his uncut hair and his abstinence from wine.

   b. Originally, the Nazirite was endowed with special charismatic gifts and normally held this status for life. Later the term was applied to a man who had voluntarily vowed to undertake special religious observances for a limited period of time, the completion of which was marked by the presentation of offerings (Numbers 6:1; Maccabees 3:49; Acts 21:24 (Britannica).

c. Samson was born during a time when Israel was in rebellion and disobedience to God and Israel could not defeat their enemy. *Note: when a Believer is in blatant disobedience, their confidence to believe God to help is rendered nil, and they are also rendered unable to face their enemy. And they are under conviction of God and the condemnation of the devil.*

d. As a foundation for Samson's story, the Philistines, Israel's enemy, ravished them of their food and livelihood for forty years. A man named Manoah of the tribe of Dan had a wife who was barren. God, in His mercy towards His people sent an angel of the Lord to speak with her and tell her some good news. This is found in (Judges 13:1-14).

e. Samson's story as a mighty warrior and judge is breath-taking. The Spirit of God would come upon Samson, and he would slay many of Israel's enemies. The story of his defeating a thousand Philistines with the jawbone of a donkey is well known (Judges 15:15-16). However, he had been instructed not to reveal the source of his power. His hair represented and manifested a glory and power from God that was unique to him. However, his failure to seek the Lord and stay close enough to the Lord to keep his vow as a Nazarite, impeded his hearing—even his logic. Lust and pride were given way to bring about separation, disregard, rebellion against God, along with intrigue, sin, shame and the loss of his hair (which was never to be cut). Lastly, came the loss of his God-given authority, power and his physical eyes (Judges 16:20-21). Though he knew what he was supposed to do, lust had taken him into her bosom and held him there lulling him into a stupor that made him momentarily forget who he was. Then lust and pride beguilingly drew out of Samson the intimate secret between him and God. This is truly disheartening, but there is a more favorable ending to Samson's story because at the end of his life he truly repented and brought down more Philistines in his death than in his lifetime, thus, fulfilling his purpose for being born.

If, we will pray to *witness* in our pure conscience what Christ did for us, with understanding we will acknowledge that when Christ died, was buried, and resurrected, we also died, was buried, and resurrected with Him and will reckon dead that nature that He took on Himself and put to death, we will grow and mature to slay every enemy *IN* us that has obstructed our Path and has caused destruction to us or others we have come in contact with. And our lives will be light, salt, and made the very life and breath of God to others.

6. Our zeal for the Lord is swallowed up

a. During this whole process of prayerlessness, the once fiery Believer becomes someone that is not distinguished them from worldliness or the worldly way of life. They have become lukewarm. It is in this state of lukewarmness that they may find themselves *turned over* to desires that they thought were long gone. And it is true that they were put to death in the death of our Lord Yeshua. However, that old man dies hard, and we are faced with it every day as to whether or not we will give our body to its *ghost, if you will,* or to the Lord.

b. There is a zeal we see in a person who has freshly given their heart and life to the Lord Yeshua. They want everyone to know who He is and what He has done for them. They are hungry for Him because they have experienced His touch and holiness. His Presence is real to them and they want to run before they have even learned to crawl or walk. They spend as much time as they can with the Lord and His word so they can fellowship with Him. This zeal is meant to mature in the Believer. And even though they are a babe, the Lord shows Himself with and through them so that they will be strengthened and encouraged to keep coming to Him and grow up in the faith.

Perhaps your zeal is swallowed up by separation, rebellion and disobedience. **Return** to the Lord and **repent**. Began to **seek the Lord in prayer again** and believe that the One who loved you then, still loves you now. He will restore His Vision for your life and He will help you to find where you placed your zeal, revive it, that He may be glorified in it. Our zeal for Him is what will take us through the jubilant times as well as the tough ones…and with joy.

Prayerlessness is a death to the Christ-Believer. Let me explain it this way: While life is going well, many of us have gone for days, weeks or months without fervent, consistent prayer and fellowship with the Lord. It's like we are saying to the Lord, "I got it!" But when things fall apart, we fall on our faces crying out to Him to get us out of the conflict. We feel condemned and do not always have the confidence that He will answer us because we know we have neglected or betrayed Him. This crying out and fellowship should be a daily consistent thing along with fellowship because we do not know what a day holds, and we need His abundant love, grace, mercy and closeness.

While prayerlessness is a death to the Believer, effective, fervent, and consistent prayer is life. It awakens a desire for greater fellowship with the Lord. We receive confidence to approach Him, and it moves the Lord to answer us, to quicken or make alive His word in us or whatever we need.

CHAPTER (13)

The Power of Prayer

When we accept the sacrifice of Yeshua and receive Him as Lord and Savior of our lives, He truly cleanses us from the original sin of Adam and our sins which we have sinned in our bodies. And true to this marvelous encounter with the Almighty, we begin to see the world differently as well as people. Though we are truly babes in Him, we find that there is now a different conscience and consciousness that was not there before.

This brings me to the time when I was attending the community college in my home town. Someone put my name in as a candidate to run for home-coming queen (to this day I still don't know who). By some grace of God, I won. Shortly afterwards, I think that night, the college had a party for all of the guys who were a part of the basketball team and the homecoming lineup. When the dance was on, I started dancing with one of the team players (I loved to dance and still think it is a beautiful form of art).

But all of a sudden, I felt convicted, out of place and I could not stay. I finished that dance, but shortly after that, I left. There was nothing wrong with that dance, but for that time in my life as a very young follower of Christ, I was in the process of changing dance partners. And the Lord was awakening a conscience and consciousness in me that He would one day give me a greater understanding of.

Now I do believe in the power of the sent preacher because that person that is sent of God to minister the words of life to us, has been broken by the Lord, is not a novice, and has dealt with much of what we face in our life journey. Many of these sent ones are like fathers and mothers to us and will be merciful and prayerful towards us while we grow up in the faith. As long as they follow the Lord, we need their counsel and godly example. And prayerfully, the things they teach us will have great weight in how we live in and out of their presence.

We should beware of being too quick to think that we have grown beyond them. For example, 2 Chronicles 24 tells the story of Joash, who was only seven years old when he became king. There was a godly priest in his life named Jehoiada. While Jehoiada lived, Joash lived for God and did what was right. His heart was set on repairing the Lord's House. Unfortunately, when Jehoiada died, so did the things he taught Joash—who was quick to abandon his quest for the House of God, and he turned away from the God of his fathers and served Asherah and idols.

Thus, the sent preacher gently pushes us towards our destiny, constantly counsels us, is used by God to keep us on a straight path and help us to leap over obstacles in a considerably shorter period of time that might take us 40 years scraping to do it on our own. Besides, Yeshua showed us this pattern of discipleship with those He trained.

When we find the power that is in prayer, those things that are deeply rooted and hidden in us, such as anger, hurt, bitterness, deceitfulness, deceptive ways, murder, unfaithfulness, fornication, adultery, strife, witchcraft, envying, drunkenness and the like (Galatians 5), can be plucked up, removed and cleansed from us as we seek the Lord to bring us to a healthy and whole state (spirit, soul, mind, body and purse). There are things we don't even know are in us until the Lord brings it to the surface, or our buttons are pushed. We are appalled at ourselves and want to run and hide. And there are things we may never know was in us because the Lord, in His mercy eradicates some of those things at the point of new birth or during the processes of our growth. Again, we have these undesirable traits because we were born human and certain things or entities attached themselves to each individual at birth or as a child in greater or lesser degrees. But the born-again Believer is not a better person than the one who has not yet received Christ, however, there is a distinction; the Believer has entered into a powerful Covenant, that if understood, they can learn to walk as the original Man/Woman God made. This is wonderful to me!

Prayer has the power to touch the heart of the Living God to cause those things that are evil in us to be shaken loose and fall away. If we say we have no problems in us, we are truly liars and deceive ourselves and make it difficult to receive the help of God. If we find it difficult to say, "I am sorry, I was wrong, or forgive me for hurting you," we may very well be clogged up with our own trash and polluted with it. Yet still, if there is life in us, the merciful and loving God will forgive the one who comes to Him in repentance and cleanse them from all unrighteousness (1 John 1:9).

When my children were small, I told them many stories around the table before bedtime. I also endeavored to teach them prayer and the Armor of God. In most cases they cooperated with me during our prayer times. But there was one particular day when it was tough to teach them. That day I walked away frustrated with them. But the truth was, it was I who was frustrating the Lord, who was wooing and leading me into a deeper prayer life, but I was fighting Him just like my children were fighting me. I finally gave in and started yielding and consistently spending quality time with the Lord.

In those early years the Lord was so patient and kind and dealt with me tenderly. I began to see and understand Him better and He was gracious to answer me. Furthermore, when I was going astray from His path, He spoke to me so tenderly about my error, it could have broken my bones because He made me 'see' how deeply I grieved Him. This season of prayer went on for years. The Lord used me and gave me a ministry where He made me profitable to His work. This took place until certain issues in our family life that were not faced and properly dealt with came to the surface. Devastating things happened, our family was broken, and a long season of wandering and captivity took place in my life—20 years!

Despite all those things, the Lord never left me. (I'm so grateful!) The spirit of prayer never left me. I truly believe that because the Lord helped me to keep that connection between us, I never felt totally disconnected from Him, though some of the things I was going through were *unspeakable*. Even in my great immaturity, He was working in my life. In my arrogance and pride He was working in my life. Oh, how I thought I'd arrived in those early days. But I was just a suckling babe on milk. I did not realize how much 'law' or self-righteousness was in me. It could have killed a mighty man of valor. It took going through those many heartaches, maltreatment, trials, sin and grievances, all the way to New Jerusalem Church, just to be able to truly begin to look at and see myself as the wretch I am (apart from Christ).

It has been over seven years since I first met Apostle Perry and the now late Pastor Shackleford. We hardly completed a service without the encouragement of growing in our prayer lives. I watched Apostle Perry pray for people, and I was in awe of the Lord. People were delivered of demons, healed in their bodies, as well as received words that changed their lives forever. Sometimes just sitting in the Presence of the Lord was a life-changer.

I remember when I first started attending New Jerusalem Church, there was an individual who was very sick. During the first year there, I watched this person receive prayer again and again. Their healing was not immediate to the naked eye, but they did recover through the power of prayer. It was wondrous to behold. Seeing this on a weekly basis, several times a week imprinted a new desire to walk in righteousness, holiness and to be a person that the Lord could call on to pray once again.

In October of 2022, I was on a visit with my Dad for a few days. During my visit, two of my nieces and their children stopped in to spend time with him too. We all had a very sweet time together. During our conversation, one of my nieces, Dannyell, told us of a friend of hers who was living in a foreign country completing a very important project. One day her friend came to her heart in an urgent manner. This continued throughout the day: and as he came to her heart, she prayed in the urgency she felt. She knew something was wrong, and felt he was not safe. He was not answering his phone as he normally would. Some days later, he reached out to her to tell her that he had been robbed. The robbers took everything: his information, phone, his money, his belongings. They had guns, machetes, small knives, and other weapons. However, *they looked on him strangely*—all of them! But they did not kill him, though they wanted too. They just kept looking at him. Then they finally left. When he reported what had happened to his fellow workers that were natives of that land, they were shocked. They could only say, "How are you still here? You should be dead. They don't leave people alive. How are you still here?" My niece has learned something important: when someone comes to your heart in such an urgent manner, pray! And even if it does not seem urgent, it is better to pray for people who come to our hearts.

I read an article called, "The Prayer Pocket." It shared 10 benefits of prayer:
1. Prayer draws us close to God:
   a. As we draw close, our hearts get tender and pride begins to fall away
   b. The Lord is near to all who call on Him in truth (Psalm 145:18)
   c. The Lord does not leave us hanging; He tells us to draw near to Him and He will draw near to us. (James 4:8).
2. Prayer shapes our hearts:
   a. The Lord truly can give a new heart and cleans us from a stony one (Ezekiel 36:26).
3. Prayer grows our trust
   a. As we continue to come to the Lord, He reveals Himself the more. His character and His word become something we trust
4. Prayer provides guidance:
   a. We are admonished as well as encouraged to acknowledge the Lord in all our ways and He will direct our paths (Proverbs 3:6).
5. Prayer gives us perspective:
   a. Sometimes through prayer, I have been made able to see something from someone else's eyes and have understanding or just be merciful.
6. Prayer calms our heart and mind:
   a. The Lord knows how to give us comfort and peace when we go to Him and cast our cares on Him.
7. Prayer conforms our will to God's Will:
   a. The plans and vision the Lord has for us will become ours when we ask for His will in our lives. Our calling and elections become clearer and will come to fruition.
8. Prayer makes us more like Jesus:
   a. The Believer in Christ is destined to be conformed to His image
   b. (Romans 8:29) As we yield our bodies to His will, we are transformed from the inside out.

9. Prayer leads us to forgiveness:
    a. Oh how we need forgiveness and the grace to forgive. Prayer will help us to tear down our inward laws that says, "That person has wronged me and deserves to pay or be condemned."
    b. To release someone of a sin or wrong is not always easy, but it denotes a grace and power that we cannot claim as our own. When a grudge is held for a long time, the person's heart could be very hard. But God can massage the grudge out and dispel its power, remove the heart of stone and give a new tender   one.
    Furthermore, tenderness of heart will lead us to repentance, not only initially, but all along our journey of life with the Lord.
10. Prayer sets our minds on things above.

There have been occasions when after my prayer time I got distracted, and the blessing from that time was not able to carry me through my day. Those days were almost always "off". Then there are those times when I have had an awesome prayer, and my heart and mind are filled with the things the Lord ministered or His Presence would linger on me throughout the day. My mind was not cluttered and I felt the cleansing that took place with Him. My focus remained on Him and the life I have in Him. Furthermore, in those moments my conscience served me in the smallest of things. Sincere prayer sets our focus on the matters of God and helps us to deal with the things we are daily confronted with in our lives. Prayer does work. And God does answer prayer.

CHAPTER (14)

The Discipline

Another thing that occurred during that long season of prayer, the Lord ministered to me about what He referred to as, *The Discipline of Faithfulness*. His purpose and intent was to bring my life into a place where prayer, fellowship and the word would encompass the whole of my life and draw me closer to Him, thus, being the center of my life or the core of my activity. It was meant to affect everything about me in a way that will allow me to grow up properly and increase in faith, virtue and the knowledge of God.

At the onset of my new birth, the Lord literally cleansed me of a foul and perverse, unruly mouth. It was gone!!! This was a life-changer because at that time, I was given to a short temper. When my buttons were pushed I could not control my tongue. Because of this miracle in my young teenage life, I knew I had encountered the power of the Most High. The 'color' of the world around me changed. I didn't see things quite the same. Yes, I was a babe in Christ that had many issues, but the Lord was working in me His Will. And what happened to me was something I had never experienced before. My life was being transformed. When I became oppressed by my flesh nature or weighted down with the threat of depression, I would refer back to that powerful time, especially when I needed answers to prayer.

Then the Lord began to deal with my eating habits. I must say, I enjoyed food (especially cheeseburgers). As a young teen, my appetite was ferocious. And this entered into my young adulthood. The Lord took me off pork and then for seasons at a time, off of beef. Though from time to time I will eat beef, it is seldom that I will go to the store and buy it, because now I rarely get a taste for it. The Lord also took me through times of fasting with prayer. I saw my appetite take a turn to better and healthier eating. Furthermore, the Lord dealt with me concerning the words that came forth out of my mouth. This proverb was at work in me, to not speak evil of anyone. *"If I could not speak something good, don't speak at all."* Years later and at this present season, this was reintroduced and reinforced at New Jerusalem Church. Now the discipline of being conscious of every thought that comes to me is underway and at work in my life. I have a different understanding about this now because the kind of exercising this requires in 'conscience' to deal with myself does not afford me the energy of constantly pointing my finger at someone else's error. I must always look at and deal with the ugly things in my life. In our church life we are learning to bring the pieces together through prayer so that our conscience will serve us in all things that we may learn to operate in our new nature.

I have heard Apostle/Pastor Perry talk about this and it is true: There are so many disciplines in the world. And when it comes to religious disciplines, those that take care to bring their bodies in alignment and free from the things that Paul talks about in Galatians 5:19-21, do well. We are admonished that there are things that should not be even named among us as followers of Christ (Ephesians 5:3). Thus, in that respect, there are those different religious disciplines that should make the average Christian really look at what they believe because some of these disciplines put Christianity to shame. Not because I think they are better, or the truest discipline of the follower of Christ is not up to par, but because on an average the things the Christian church has allowed up this point are against what we *say* we believe in the holy scriptures. I mean no harm. I know the wretchedness of my flesh nature.

Now let's look at just three of the disciplines that mark certain religions. I will also talk about a Catholic Priest and his life as Benedictine monk:

A. Jainism: Jainism, mostly an Indian religion, is counted as one of the oldest belief systems in the world and has 4.2 million followers.

Jainism is a religion of self-help. They do not believe in a creator God, but <u>each Jain believes that they can obtain the status of god if they practice right faith, right knowledge, and right conduct</u>. They believe that this kind of living will rid their souls of karma, resulting in a pure, omniscient, and perfectly happy soul.

Jains have 24 Tirthankaras (teachers) who they believe have achieved perfection. According to them, these teachers appear in the world to lead others to the way of Moksha (or freedom from reincarnation). They do not worship a god or gods, but do pay homage to the Tirthankaras because they believe that they represent the purest developed state of the soul.

Jains live in isolated groups or communities. And because of their <u>fundamental belief in non-violence, they are of the strictest of vegetarians (excluding all meat and eggs</u>. Thus, the serious Jain in their pursuit of perfection will adhere to five vows:

1. (Ahimsa)--To <u>cause no harm to other human beings, as well as all living beings (particularly animals).</u>
   This is the highest ethical duty in Jainism. It is also demanded of the Jain to be non-violent in one's speech and thoughts.

2. (Satya)--This is a vow that the Jain will make to
   <u>always speak the truth</u>. They won't lie and will not
   encourage or approve anyone who will speak
   untruths.
3. (Asteya)--This is the <u>vow to not steal</u>. The Jain
   layperson should not take anything that is not
   willingly given. Additionally, a Jain mendicant
   (beggar) should ask for permission to take it if
   something is being given.
4. (Brahmacharya)--This is the vow of <u>celibacy</u>. The
   Jain practices abstinence from sex and sensual
   pleasures is prescribed for Jain monks and nuns. For
   the layperson, this vow means chastity or
   faithfulness to one's partner.
5. (Aparigraha)--This is a <u>vow of "non-
   possessiveness</u>." It speaks of non-attachment to
   material and psychological possessions, to avoid
   craving and greed. The Jain monks and nuns
   completely renounce property and social relations,
   owning nothing and are attached to no one. This is
   not altogether true for the layperson. Though they
   may hold to possessions 'loosely', some of the Jains
   are wealthy.

B. **Buddhist Belief**: The following are considered the
Foundation of Buddhism's Four noble truths:
1. The truth of suffering ("dukkha")
2. The truth of the cause of suffering ("samudaya")
3. The truth of the end of suffering ("nirhodha")
4. The truth of the path that frees us from suffering
   ("magga")

Buddhism had five precepts that all Buddhists endeavor
to follow:

a. Do not harm or kill living things

b. Do not take things unless they are freely given.
c. Lead a decent life.
d. Do not speak unkindly or tell lies.
e. Do not abuse drugs or drink alcohol.

<u>Meditation is an essential practice to most Buddhists</u>. It helped them to look within themselves as they sought enlightenment from the truths of Buddha's teaching. And furthermore, meditation has been known to assist individuals to explore their own spirituality. It also has these proven benefits:

- Increases self-awareness
- Helps with focus and concentration
- Reduces stress
- Increases emotional strength
- Helps with memory
- Promotes better decision-making skills
- Promotes better sleep
- Boosts immune health
- Slows aging

Buddha, (or Siddhartha Gautama) was a prince who grew up knowing the palace life in North India, in what is known today as Nepal. As he grew he up and engaged in the environment around him, he sought to understand and find answers to the questions he faced in his life. His royal life was a luxurious one, and he questioned his sheltered life. He decided to explore the lives of the people apart from what he had been accustomed to. During a time after he left the palace, he saw four things: a sick man, an old man, a dead man and a monk. From these sights he understood that not even his position as a prince could make him escape illness, suffering and death. However, it was the sight of the monk that encouraged him to leave his life as a royal and become a wandering holy man who was seeking answers to his questions like, "Why must people suffer?" What is the cause of suffering?" Siddhartha spent the better part of his life practicing prayer, meditation and fasting until he understood what he came to know as his teaching called, "the basic truths of life." This event occurred after he had sat under a Poplar-fig tree for many days in deep meditation. With this enlightenment (or nirvana) he gained, he was given the title of Buddha. Buddha means Enlightened One. Buddhists follow a path of moral living, thinking and behavior, as well as seeking wisdom, And the precepts that Buddhist adhere to is what causes Buddhists to refrain from killing, stealing, lying, misusing sex, or using drugs or alcohol. It is said that Buddha lived to be 80 years. And I will add, there are also believing Christians who practice meditation and have learned to keep the victory over their lives.

C. Islamic Belief: The five pillars and the core beliefs of Islam goes like this:

    a. Profession of Faith (shahada). The belief that "There is no god but God, and Muhammad is the Messenger of God" is central to Islam.

    b. Prayer (salat). Muslims pray facing Mecca five times a day: at dawn, noon, mid-afternoon, sunset, and after dark...

    c. Alms (zakat)...

    d. Fasting (sawm)...

    e. Pilgrimage (hajj)...

Islam has two major sects, (Sunnis and Shiites) and 90% are Muslims and are known as Sunnis. Muslims pray five times a day to remind them of the existence of the supreme beings, their creator, the owner of this universe and all of their possessions, even their life. They offer prayer to make themselves more submissive and increase their belief that there is a substance higher than themselves. Islam believes that there is One, Unique, Incomparable God, who has no son or partner. According to them, Allah is the proper name of god. "The God." And their belief in prophets of God include the following: Adam, Noah, Ishmael, Issac, Jacob, Moses, Jesus (Yeshua) and the Final Prophet and Messenger, Muhammad. Also, there is a belief in the Day of Judgment: When all of humanity will be held accountable for their deeds. They hold to a belief in the Angels of God, belief in "Qadar" Predestine (fate or divine foreordainment and divine decree) and Due Measure (occurrence of events according to predefined measures, standards or criteria), innocence of humankind at birth and no intermediary between God and humans.

Father Karl Barmann, OSB

On January 19, 2023, I interviewed Father Karl W. Barmann, a local Catholic priest in our community. He agreed to speak with me and allowed me to interview him concerning the life and discipline of one of their nuns. Previously, when we first made contact on phone, I inquired about speaking to one of their nuns concerning their prayer discipline. And his answer was that he could tell me about that himself. I wasn't sure how he could tell me about the private disciple of the nun, but I agreed to his wishes and would soon understand his statement. When our interview began, I learned that he felt the call of God to the priesthood as a young person. He also told me that he was a Benedictine *monk* in his priesthood. This greatly stirred my interest, because I had also been searching in the city for a monk to speak with about their discipline of life.

Just for the sake of the understanding for the reader, Britannica online, gives a brief description of this order as follows:

Benedictine, member of the Order of Saint Benedict (O.S.B.), member of any of the confederated congregations of monks, lay brothers, and nuns who follow the rule of life of St. Benedict (*c.* 480–*c.* 547) and who are spiritual descendants of the traditional monastics of the early medieval centuries in Italy and Gaul. The Benedictines, strictly speaking, do not constitute a single religious order, because each monastery is autonomous (or have the right or power of self-government).

- The Benedictine monk (as well as the nun) takes a vow of the following:
- Obedience
- Poverty
- Chastity
- Conversion of life, and
- Stability

According to Father Karl, a Benedictine monk does what he refers to as "prayer and work." This phrase is also found on the emblem of Billimoria High School in Panchgani, India. The phrase pray and work (or 'pray and labor'; Latin: ora et labora) refers to the Catholic monastic practice of working and praying, generally associated with its use in the Rule of Saint Benedict.

As a routine schedule of their daily life, they seek God through the tools and helps of the "Divine Office" (this can be found online). They pray five (5) times a day as a community of brothers. They gather in the church to administer the office of readings, morning prayers (lauds), noon-day prayers, evening prayers (vespers), and night prayers (compline). Furthermore, Father Karl explained it this way, "Benedictine monks live in the community seeking God in the community of their brothers in order to better serve that community".

As far as Father Karl's early life is concerned, he grew up on a farm. It was hard work, but it paid the bills. It didn't make them rich, but they were not poor. He grew up with five brothers and three sisters. One of his sisters is a nun, who performed the same vows as Rev. Karl. She has served the Lord in her ministry as a teacher. He also had a cousin, a Jesuit in the ministry along with other relatives that encouraged him by their way of life in the ministry.

Father Karl is also a veteran. He was a Chaplain soldier in the Air Force. As an Air Force chaplain, he committed himself to 19 assignments over different parts of the world for 28 years, starting as a lieutenant and ending his military chaplaincy career as a Colonel. His career as a Benedictine priest spans 57 years. And he has been serving at St Joseph Catholic Church as their pastor since 2018 and publishes a weekly "Pastor's Reflection" in the news section.

Father Karl feels that the life he is living is a gift. He admonishes us in this way, *"Live content with what you have. Find happiness with who you are. Don't get attached to things. Seek God as your attachment, seeking His will for your life."* Rev. Barmann has truly learned to be content in whatsoever state he finds himself. And the Lord has taken him places he never saw himself going and doing things he did not even dream of doing. It was a blessing to be in his presence and encounter his sincerity in his service to the Lord.

Deacon Jethro Williams

It is difficult for me to just go on and not share with you the little I know about my paternal grandfather, Jethro Williams (PawPaw).

From a small child until my preteens, I was blessed to spend time with him. PawPaw was a very quiet man. However, I remember him standing up and sharing the Sunday School lessons in church. He was very passionate and loud *when it came to that*, and he always sounded like the old-time preachers. PawPaw was no-nonsense too. He said what he meant, and he meant what he said. He smiled often, but he was temperate and truthful.

One day I made a cake; I'll admit, it did look a little lopsided and overcooked to me even at that time. I was not yet experienced with baking and just starting out, but I wanted to share a piece of it with PawPaw. I cut him a big slice. He gladly received it. And when I saw him some few days later, I asked, "PawPaw, how did you like the cake?" He gently replied, "It wasn't good. I didn't like it!" Well, I was shocked to say the least, but in my heart, I held a respect for him that has lasted to this day. And because he was so honest with me, I knew I could trust him.

PawPaw was always a godly man in my eyes, but the one thing I was not aware of until my grown-up years, was his prayer life. He was said to be, not only a man of prayer, but a man that God heard and answered. Men of God (the Cloth) would go to him for prayer—and God answered those prayers. In his prayer discipline, he prayed much for his children and grandchildren. I feel that I am a product of God answering PawPaw's prayers.

These religious and individual disciplines speak volumes concerning people; some, who by their strength and power, live decent and moral lives, and some who depend on the power of God. It is a good to have some laws in place in order to govern the body, however, we need grace to approach God and be empowered to live right and be able to know and walk out our eternal destiny.

At the beginning of Mr. Johnson's memoir, he spoke of taking very few belongings with him because he knew that becoming a soldier meant he would be changed into another person. There is a depth to what he said. He was leaving behind what he knew of his old life and embarking and embracing the new one he was running towards.

Furthermore, he would have to let go of his mindset to embrace one that would help him to become a disciplined soldier.

2 Corinthians 5:17 reads like this, *"If any man be in Christ, he is a new creation. Old things have passed away. Behold, all things are become new."* When I think about the Mind of Christ, I know that it is the very Mind of God the Father. As Believers, we have access by grace to His Mind...if we will allow. We are transformed by the renewing of our minds. When I hear the preached word, my mind is renewed, when I turn it over, it is renewed, and when I pray it is renewed and often I witness a change, a transformation has taken place in me because the Lord gave me increase on the word that was ministered. Accordingly, our new creation is made with another heart in a quickened spirit (Ephesians 2). The heart of humanity is deceitful above all things and desperately wicked: Who can know it (Jeremiah 17:9)? Thus, instead of the foreskin of the Israelite males being circumcised in the Covenant of the Law, our hearts are circumcised (the removal of the cold, dead, stone-like calloused stiff-neckedness against the Lord) through sanctification in the New Covenant. We are given a new heart that can respond to the Lord as we reach out to Him as our All in All. Additionally, our new creation is "light." Yes, our New Creation is Light! On the mountain, Yeshua revealed this when He was transfigured before the disciples who went with Him there (Matthew 17:1-3). And His life is in us because we have been quickened from the dead.

The quiet place with the Lord is a space where all the hustle and bustle is shut out. It is a place where we can learn to get past ourselves and receive an ear that can hear. In that place, the Lord's transformative power is revealed. He shows us the things that we sometimes already know we need to deal with, and things we are not aware that we need to correct. He sometimes does operations in us. And in this place, we learn His discipline. In the quiet consciousness of the Lord, battles in us are won. And because the battle is won from within, change will manifest outwardly.

CHAPTER (15)

Study Me/Study the Word

*Study to shew thyself approved unto God, a workman that needeth not to be ashamed, rightly dividing the word of truth (*2 Timothy 2:15 kjv).

Need not to be ashamed...

I watched a group of children do their various scenes in a darling children's play. Some had special singing parts, while others sang and danced. Some knew their parts well; they were very confident and did not miss a beat. However, it was painfully noticeable that some of the children did not know their parts. In uncomfortable movements they scrambled and faked it to get through. This is interesting to me.

How many times have we done something that we had not worked out the kinks? How many times have we stood in front of people and were not prepared? Whether, group-sharing, teaching, singing, work-related, whatever it may be? And how many times have we stood before people who needed to hear a word or song with the anointing of God's approval, but we came up short? In those times we walk away knowing we did not prepare ourselves properly in the presence of God, in our study, or our prayer. Or we may have tried to share something we have not yet witnessed and proved in our lives. Even David refused Saul's armor that he had not yet proved (1 Samuel 17:38). If we don't do like David did with Saul's (unproved) armor, in our time to shine for the Lord, we will walk away ashamed.

Gamaliel was a teacher of the Law of Moses. He was well respected, honored, and was the teacher by whom Paul the Apostle sat under tutelage. As a master of the Law, Gamaliel was considered one of the greats. He knew the Law and studied it in great detail. And when the early disciples were preaching Jesus and persecuted by the leaders of the Jews for their testimony, Gamaliel did not shake hands with the evil they were doing to the disciples. He counseled them to be careful how they treated the disciples. He told them that if the work of these men was not of God, it would come to nothing. However, if it be of God, they would not be able to overthrow it and they would become as those who were fighting against God (Acts 5:34-39). He knew that there was a possibility that Yeshua could have truly been the One/the Messiah who was to come, and was not willing to raise his hand against those that may be carrying the Torch of God for the One they claimed to be waiting for. Gamaliel could not have withstood those who opposed the disciples unless he was a man of prayer. He was not going to miss out. He studied to show himself approved to God. And he was not going to be ashamed. May we honor the Lord and pray (and get an answer) before we raise our voice to speak out against someone, or use our influence to strike anyone that claims to know the Lord, but does not look like us, talk like us, or keep company with us.

As I trust the Lord in the study of me and His word, there is a growing love and appreciation of my life in and with Him. *I am loved.* This is a most cherished understanding and an ongoing experience. And the love back to Him is received. He is teaching me contentment, to be His woman and His soldier. This contentment is also a guard and covering from the lust of the eye that can never be satisfied. Now, growing in this contentment, I appreciate others and what they have been given from above, but don't want to copy them because the Lord has invested in me and has His own expression through my body. This contentment makes me ever grateful for what the Lord has accomplished in my life at this juncture. And when He is moving forward, I want to move with Him to the next place of contentment. Though the soldier's life is not always an easy one, there is a joy in being His righteousness. No other life can give this to us. This life in Christ is teaching me a lifetime of warfare that I did not expect...the warfare of the destruction (or reckoning dead) of the old me...that I be not ashamed, being one who confesses Him as Lord and Savior.

Studying me...

Knowing and understanding me has been and is an adventure (downhill and uphill). With all due respect, when I was growing up, I was taught, in a decent, yet intentional way to be a "Pleaser." I will dare say that there are some features to the Pleaser that can be appealing, but in some cases, the person can grow up at the feet of Fear and at the expense of their soul. Moreover, the Pleaser may not know themselves because they have spent so much of their lives being busy to please someone else. In marriage, pleasing the one you love is a beautiful thing, (if not against the conscience) however, it can be a problem when those two people become "one", but have not taken the time to know and understand themselves. When we look at some of the manifestations of the Pleaser it can be disheartening. Some of them include the following:

- Pretending to agree with everyone
- Feeling responsible for how other people feel
- Apologizing often
- Feeling burdened by the things you have to do
- Can't say no

- Feeling uncomfortable if someone is angry with you
- Act like the people around you
- The need of praise to feel good
- Go through great lengths to avoid conflict
- Not truthful when your feelings are hurt

Though I did not display all of these manifestations, I recognize several of them. However, I smile in appreciation because these things that have manifested out of me, I am witnessing them put to death.

When I became a part of the church in North Carolina, I had, as I shared earlier, to be healed inwardly and to be healthy and whole. In the process of this healing, there was an awakening or revealing that my then "age-maturity" did not have a match for the emotional, psychological and spiritual aspects of my life. I saw great immaturity in me and the need to grow up. I had seen bits and pieces of this about myself during those dark years. But here, my deficiency could not be hidden any longer.

The late Pastor Patricia Shackleford was a marvelous leader. She was wise, beautiful, very brilliant, and a wealthy woman. When she first came to New Jerusalem, she was someone that was different from the norm. She saw the need of the people there. She saw the need of the women there. She could see the women who were at the mercy of their own insufficiencies. And she saw the harsh reality of women who were totally dependent on someone else to survive. She was completely for men, but she endeavored to teach the women, (younger and older) of our church to be able to take care of themselves: go to school, get degrees of your choice, get a good job, buy your own car(s), buy your own home(s), get to know yourself, and if you have a desire to marry, live by yourself for a while before marrying. She also taught the men of our church as well. And was mentor to our presiding leader. She was a teacher of the whole church. Anyone who listened to her and followed her instructions, did not fail, but had successful outcomes. Pastor Shackleford never married. She was a successful and well-traveled business woman. However, she left her secular work and dedicated her life to the work of the Lord, to serve Him and equip His people. Though I got in on the back end of this, (three years with her), her soft-spoken voice is loud and clear in me to do in my life as an older woman, what was not accomplished in my earlier years. Because of these leaders, I can see a restoration of prayer and a love for the study of the word of God returning with fire.

Amongst the countless   Spirit and life teachings we receive, Apostle/Pastor Perry ministers to us to study and know ourselves. As a very young person, I initially did not want to marry. After the Lord saved me, I contemplated being a nun. But decided that I wanted my own house and vehicle and a good job to carry me while I pursued a Gospel singing career. Instead, I married young, and not much later, started having children. Because I had not taken the time to live by myself, I really did not know myself.

As a new disciple of the ministry at New Jerusalem Church, we were taught the word. After hearing it, we learned to follow it up by turning it over and praying over what has been taught. Prior to this ministry, I heard the preached word, tried to retain what I had heard, but because I sometimes listened to too many teachers, I went off on my own thoughts or tangent and did not always stay within the boundaries or concentrate in a singular manner on what was ministered at that time. In doing it my way, the spirit of what was taught could only penetrate my heart to a degree. Furthermore, in my life, many pieces of the Gospel were still scattered. Despite my deficiencies, the Lord graciously used me, knowing He would later bring me to greater understanding.

I must tell you, before becoming a part of New Jerusalem, no one else made me look at and study my *movements*, or study the 'spirit' of my words, my thoughts, and take authority over my own body and make it obey me unto righteousness. We are regularly admonished to daily examine ourselves and to exercise our pure conscience that will only lead us to do what is right.

Moreover, no one else made me look into the ministry of Perfection that is a part of the ministry of the Lord Jesus. Now, when the spirit of my words are not right, or my thoughts are evil, my conscience is greatly pricked, and I am moved to acknowledge it because the Spirit of God who indwells me will make me deal with unrighteousness in me (my members), and reckon it dead through the finished work of Christ. And as previously stated, this purged conscience resides in a brand new born-again Believer, (it was in me) but if it is not developed with teaching, in most cases we will began to flow with the norm of what is happening in our environment amongst other Believers.

Studying the Word...Be still and know...

During those early years when I was first born again, the word of God was food to me. It was like water in the desert, and I loved opening its pages. The love I had for it was a gift and I was often drawn to read and study. In my reading time, I made a point to memorize a large portion of it. At that time, it was a joy to find and link the passages for understanding. When the Lord gave revelation, it gave me such peace and joy. The Lord was faithful to meet with me, however, at different stages I was trying to do too much on my own. And some of those years, instead of having too many teachers, I did not have a teacher. It's not that the Lord did not give me understanding of things when I sought Him for it, but my progress was not always steady, and I was distinctly aware that there were still many pieces that I did not have in place for understanding my calling and election or what the Lord has given to us who believe and trust in His finished work. Little by little, I am experiencing a wholeness, which is something awesome and unfamiliar. By the grace of the Lord, I am now learning to live out the marriage of God's word and prayer.

When we hear the sent preacher minister the word, it is our responsibility to receive it in the spirit it was given and likewise, read, meditate on it and study it. I still love simply reading the word of God. And sometimes I get so involved in it, I feel like I am there with those people. I am weeping with them or laughing with them in their joy, or get angry or sad when someone has been dealt with wrongfully. Moreover, I still enjoy word-study and going from one applicable scripture to another. But I know that there is no revealing or unveiling of the word unless the Holy Spirit interprets the scriptures and makes them life to us. The Spirit of God has to give the increase or understanding (1 Corinthians 3:7). And there is no application of them unless the Spirit of God causes us to see, to know, that we might do and be. And according to Yeshua's more excellent pattern of discipleship, there is no putting the pieces of His Gospel together progressively with steady growth unless there is someone who is following the Lord to help us along our path, as we follow their lead. This way of study has been most profitable for me, but not easily embraced at first.

As for meditation in those early days, I remember praying at my chair and then I would get quiet so the Lord could speak to me. On one occasion in a quiet moment, He gave me almost a whole song in that setting called, "The Bigness of My God." I could see my children as a part of that song. And later on, that song was finally recorded with my children. Moreover, I did not know to call it meditation when I would be quiet and wait to hear, but it was a type of meditation in the form of very still listening. Thus, there is a meditation that goes on when we will sit, be still and let the Lord speak back His word to us. This also happens when the word is turned over. It becomes a part of you when this happens. And when the Lord speaks back His word to you and you hold on to it, no one will take its life from you. It becomes a part of the fibers of your internal being.

Someone that crossed my path years ago said something that I thought could be profitable concerning encouragement in the study of God's word. They said, "People over different parts of the world go to school to get educated to do all sorts of things and find expertise in their professions. Likewise, the follower of Christ should be an *expert* in the Word of God." I can hear this, and say, Amen. But allow me to add, if the Believer will not be an expert in God's word, at least let them know the scriptures in order to not err in them (Matthew 22:29).

CHAPTER (16)

The Consecrated Life

Take my life and let it be
Consecrated, Lord, to Thee
Take my moments and my days
Let them flow in endless praise,
Let them flow in endless praise.

Take my hands and let them move
At the impulse of Thy love.
Take my feet and let them be,
Swift and beautiful for Thee,
Swift and beautiful for Thee.

Take my voice and let me sing
Always, only, for my King.
Take my lips and let them be
Filled with messages from Thee,
Filled with messages from Thee.
This beautiful song was written by Frances R. Havergal.
(The first three stanzas)

In one of our previous chapters we talked about Samson, the Judge. From the womb he was consecrated and separated to God as a Nazarite, and walked in the miraculous.

Another individual, Samuel, lived a life of consecration to the Lord. He became a faithful priest and judge of the Lord's people. In fact, Samuel was the last judge before King Saul was put in place as the first King of Israel.

Before Samuel came into the world, his mother, Hannah, was barren and suffered ridicule and shame for her barrenness (1 Samuel 1:6). In that time, it was considered a disgrace for a man or a woman (especially the woman) to not have the capability of fecundity or having the ability to abundantly procreate. In the scriptures, procreation is considered a blessing. Thus, the inability to reproduce was also considered a curse and regarded as a punishment. If you have ever read of Michal, the daughter of King Saul and the wife of David, you may remember that she was stricken with barrenness because she despised King David in her heart as he joyously danced before the Lord with all of his might when the Ark of Covenant was returned home to its rightful place. She felt that David shamelessly uncovered himself of his kingly apparel before the women and all the people, and she told him the same (2 Samuel 6:20-23). Furthermore, children are considered a blessing and a heritage of the Lord (Psalm 127:3-5), and they remain a blessing in our New Covenant.

Hannah experienced the grief and agony of childlessness. In her pain she cried out to the Lord...specifically for a male child. She promised God that she would give the child back to the Lord if He would grant her that prayer request. The Lord granted her petition. And after she weaned Samuel, as young as he was, Hannah fulfilled her vow to dedicate him to the service of the Lord (1 Samuel Chapters 1-3). And the Lord graciously gave her more children (1 Samuel 2:21).

Samuel's life was entirely given to God and he did not deviate from the Lord all the days of his life. Additionally, it was through Samuel that the word of the Lord and open visions from God (which were rare at that time) began to flow for Israel again. Samuel's conception was fulfilled with the answer to a vow. Furthermore, in answering Hannah's request the Lord was given a faithful and *consecrated* priest who would stand in the stead of Eli and his sons (who were corrupt), and who refused to honor the Lord as a part of God's holy Levitical priesthood.

Strong's Exhaustive Concordance defines consecrated or the consecrated life in these three forms mentioned: (1) 2598 channukah (khan-oo-kaw), which means dedication, consecration. It speaks of an initiation. (2) 6942 qudash (kaw-dash), which means to be set apart or consecrated; and (3) 5144 nezer {nay'-zer}; from nazar; properly, to dedicate or something set apart, i.e. (abstractly) dedication (of a priest or Nazirite); hence (concretely) unshorn locks; also (by implication) a chaplet (especially of royalty) – consecration, crown, hair, separation. These words are strongly connected with a vow.

The Christ-Believer is part of a chosen generation, a royal priesthood and a holy nation, a peculiar people; that we should show forth the praises of Him who has called us out of darkness into His marvelous light (1 Peter 2:9). A priest's greatest responsibility is to pray and intercede according to the responsibility given them. We are separated and dedicated to the service of the Lord. Consecration can be defined as the devoting or setting apart of anything to worship or service of God. Moreover, it is not a coincidence that the life of the Believer is called to consecration as a lifestyle and or profession. Furthermore, we see the word "royal" (or crown). Through the redemptive and finished work of Yeshua, we are *made* kings and priests of our God (Revelation 1:6; 5:10). In this world we will deal with suffering of persecutions, but reigning with the Lord will follow our suffering.

Our consecration speaks of a sanctified life. When we

hear in our services, "bring our bodies under subjection," we are dealing with the sanctification of our bodies to the Lord that He might have a living sacrifice, holy to Him. (This is our responsibility) Even in the Levitical priesthood, a lame sacrifice was not acceptable.

Now, does the Lord receive us in our lameness into the Kingdom? Yes, He does! However, He is the healer of the spirit, soul, mind and body. But if we don't bring our bodies in alignment with His righteousness, we will, as Believers who have been given God's Spirit stay riddled and convulsing with our sins. In this condition, we cannot be the kind of holy sacrifice that shows forth the glory of Christ. And this being the case, it will not offer the onlooker the truest view of Yeshua, seeing our body is all they see in this world that can testify of His righteousness, mercy and love.

Our consecration is an inward separation unto the Lord. It is an inward consciousness of the Living Christ developing in us *and* into His likeness. If our inward life stays clean and free, our outer life will follow showing forth His praises. In the Old Testament when Israel was told to sanctify themselves to meet with God, the instructions were always for their outer person; They were told to wash their clothes and refrain from sexual contact with their spouses (Exodus 19:10-15). However, Yeshua gave us a perfect example when He disappeared into the wilderness, being led by the Holy Spirit to fast and pray and contend with Satan's temptations; that He might show forth the Will, the loving heart and the glory of the Father through His life. He didn't stop at the wilderness experience; His whole life was an inward fast and prayer. He had to do so that He might be able to get to each juncture before He would pay the ultimate price for our sins and iniquities. Again, He never did anything without acknowledging the Father or without the Father's approval.

CHAPTER (17)

Falling Down and Getting Back Up

This will sound strange. But when I first started attending New Jerusalem, I didn't know what to expect. I knew it was right, but it was all new. And though the Lord had placed me on a new path, I still had the memory and operations of some of the old one. During that time, much of my stay in North Carolina had the feel of whatever a *half-way house* might feel like because the Lord was freeing me of a type of prison in my mind. I fell down a lot. Watching my movements was a new thing for me and I became *raw*! It felt like being in a place stripped naked of your *familiar* clothing. But the good news was that I had to be washed and given new clothes. I am grateful!

My cousin, Dee was very sweet to me. It took six months to find a job. She fed, sheltered and clothed me like a child; though this bothered me (pride), I appreciated everything she did for me. We came to know each other better, and our fellowship carried a mutual love. When I finally got a job, it was a relief to start taking care of my personal needs and not long afterwards pay her rent. The Lord was gracious.

I had always read about Yeshua being our Advocate, but I don't remember crying out to Him to be mine. (I asked for His grace, but not His advocacy). Well, in this place, I needed his Advocacy because I was beginning to see the old me, and that me, will always make a lot of mistakes. Moreover, when you are older and dealing with things that should have been dealt with in your younger days, it is not easy. But every time the word was preached or taught, the places of immaturity in my life were being, shaken, slapped and dealt with. Some things were corrected, while others eradicated, so that my spiritual maturity could match my age-maturity and beyond. I must say, this was *very* difficult...but needed. I fell down a lot, but <u>by the grace of God</u>, I didn't quit, but kept getting up.

It had to be pride and self-righteousness in me that didn't appreciate the song that was written by Chris Tomlin and made popular by Donnie McClurkin, "We Fall Down and We Get Up." But I can say that this song now has substance and is profitable for me. It goes like this:

We fall down, but we get up
We fall down, but we get up
We fall down, but we get up
For a saint is just a sinner who fell down
But we couldn't stay there, and got up

CHAPTER (18)

The Restoration

King David's indiscretion and sin with Bathsheba and the murder of Bathsheba's husband, Uriah the Hittite, brought the never-ending sword to David's house (2 Samuel 12:10). The problems in his family became so bleak that David was, at some point dethroned by his son, Absalom, who, thirsting for the throne, schemed and stole the hearts of the men of Israel. After Absalom planned and initiated an attack against him, David had to flee the kingdom. As he went, barefoot and weeping, he became increasingly conscious of the deceitfulness of humanity, (himself included) but he could not discount the loving kindness of his God. Because David could see himself and his own mistakes in Absalom, his mercy towards Absalom was great, and he did not desire the death of his son...though Absalom's crime against his father and the kingdom was immense. Additionally, when David's troops were sent out for war against Absalom, David asked three military leaders of his army (Joab, Abishai, and Ittai) to deal tenderly with Absalom for his sake (2 Samuel 18:5). He wanted his son back home...whatever the cost. Regretfully, one of them (Joab) did not keep their word to do no harm to him, for at the first chance, Absalom was killed (murdered).

After all that Absalom did to harm his father, David's

heart still cried out to God for his son (2 Samuel 18:31-33). David was returned to his kingdom and the throne, but not without a great price. For it was through his wrong movements he came to understand the gruesome dividends of sin and the untold grace of restoration.

Joseph is another example of the restorative power of God. He was the one his brothers called, "The Dreamer." Though Rueben, the firstborn of Jacob (Israel) should have been up for the inheritance, it appeared that Jacob was set on grooming Joseph for the position. This was in the rights of the head of the household. And when we look at the Birthright (bekorah), it has to do with both position and inheritance. Thus, by birthright, the firstborn son is up for inheriting the leadership of the family and the judicial authority of his father. Furthermore, Deuteronomy 21:17 states that the son of the birthright was also entitled to a double portion of the paternal inheritance. The father also had the right, if he saw fit, to rescind the birthright and pass it on to a younger son. And in this case, Jacob was determined to groom and place Joseph in position to inherit this status.

Joseph had several dreams that revealed he would be a powerful ruler one day—even over his own family! But instead of being quiet about it, he told them the dreams. His brothers already had *beef* with him because he was their father's favorite. And to add problems to a disagreeable situation, their father gave Joseph a coat of many colors and would frequently send Joseph out (with his coat on) to check on them when they went to various places to feed their flock. Joseph was the 11th son of Jacob's twelve sons. It infuriated them that their father had given this authority to a proud little *squirt*. When they had had enough, they decided to get rid of Joseph. When on another occasion he came to check on them, they stripped his coat from him, threw him in a pit and eventually sold him into slavery. And he landed in Egypt, sold again as a slave to a man named Potiphar.

From this place, many things transpired: Though he brought blessing and prosperity to Potiphar's house, he was accused of seducing the wife of Potiphar, and placed in jail. Later, he was used to interpret the dreams of both the Cup Bearer and Chief baker of Pharaoh. His interpretations came to pass but he was forgotten for another two years. Afterwards, the Pharaoh of Egypt had two dreams that none of his magicians or wise men could interpret. Here is where the Cup Bearer of Pharaoh remembers Joseph. Joseph was brought before Pharaoh and interpreted his dreams. He warned Pharaoh that there would be seven years of plenty and seven years of famine. He continued by giving instructions to Pharaoh on what to do with the interpretation of his dreams. After which Joseph was immediately placed in a position of great authority and power directly under Pharaoh. He was given a wife and God gave him children.

The seven years of plenty went by and the seven years of famine came into place according to the interpretation of the dreams by Joseph. All the land of Egypt and around needed the surplus provided during the plentiful years. And you might have guessed it, so did Jacob's household.

When the brothers came to buy grain, that's when things got very interesting. Joseph, (whom they did not recognize) took them through a series of difficulties to make sure he could see his youngest brother Benjamin and ensure his father was still alive. He also wanted to know if his brothers were still the same character of men who sold him into bondage.

Finally, after these things, Joseph made himself known to them: the one they hated, the one they cruelly declared would never rule over them, the one they allowed their father to assume was killed by a wild beast (Genesis 37:31-34), the one they sold into slavery, and the one whom they were doing obeisance to and now ruled over them. Though they tried everything in their power to keep the words of his dream from coming to pass, they drove him into the very place the Lord would make those dreams into a reality and his destiny. Furthermore, because the Almighty placed Joseph in that Seat of Authority, they and their families would be saved and kept from starvation. The Lord, on top of giving Joseph a high position, a wife and two children, restored Joseph to his father, his brother, Benjamin, and to his other brothers. Joseph forgave them because even though they meant it for evil, God meant it for good and for restoration of lives.

The Vietnam War was considered a lost war. Because of the longevity of the war, instead of coming home in companies, our men began to come home one-by-one. While one came home, another was shipped off to war. After the Vietnam War, the longest war in American history until Afghanistan, instead of being greeted with the welcome of fanfare, parades and congratulations of their survival, these US soldiers were greeted with ridicule, being spat upon, and caused to feel shame. America did not want to have parades or congratulations for soldiers who came home from defeat. Some were torn up with their wounds, both physically and emotionally. There were even those who did not receive the care they deserved. They were met with indifference and denied GI benefits available for Vietnam veterans, and many were poverty stricken. Thus, upon returning home they received a deeper wounding because, after fighting for our country and receiving in their bodies the aftermath of war, they were put down as if they were the enemies instead of the war heroes that they truly were. Though some of the reasons for the denial of their benefits were proposed as due to stagflation and economic spiral, the promise to help these vets became for too many, nonexistent. Thus, many of those vets were broken and became homeless.

It would take nearly 20 years for America to make

restitution with the Vietnam veterans: to even first begin to say, "Thank you for your service to our country" and to help them by putting actions to their words with assistance with their physical and emotional traumatic damages incurred in war. I was thankful to read that there were vets who received benefits to help them be restored to some semblance of their former lives in the aftershock of war.

While waiting to have tires replaced on my vehicle, I met a very friendly gentleman. He began a discussion with me and another lady as we waited in the customer area of the tire shop. In conversation he casually mentioned that he was in the Vietnam War (this was not a coincidence). After about fifteen minutes, I finally ventured to question and reaffirm what he had said about being in that war. However, to my amazement, this cordial, very gentle and distinguished man immediately teared up and became choked up at the mention of it (I felt so bad for asking). By this time, the other lady had gone to pick up her vehicle. As he tried to talk to me, he fought back tears of the pain and agony that he and many of his fellow veterans had suffered during and after that war. It took him a while to share because he was visibly forcing himself not to weep. He now spends his life helping other vets get help, as well as making them aware that there is yet help to be received. I am most honored to have met him. I am thankful to our veterans who have fought on the bloody fields of war or have done their specific duties to ensure safety for our country. Their stories are important, and can bring enlightenment to us and healing to them.

Here I think about the soldier of the Lord on the battlefields of ministry; some of our missionaries have experienced the safety of God on the fields with little harm, while others have received wounds, traumas, and unspeakable experiences. Some have even given their lives so that others might hear the Gospel.

During my years in North Carolina I wept so much as I

watched what the Lord was doing for the people around me. I wept in awe of the Lord, His servants, and I wept because of my own inadequacies and wretchedness. I also wept in gratitude because He was also changing me. I continued to cry out for His restoration and His Destiny for my life.

Apostle/Pastor Perry would often say to us, *"You just don't know how much the Lord loves you."* Or he would say, *"You don't believe the Lord loves you."* That was true. At that time my confidence as a minister of the Gospel and even as a singer was very small. My faith was little. Reluctantly, in retrospect, I finally admitted in my heart that I didn't believe the Lord loved me very much. I felt I was damaged goods and not worth much. And it was because of God's grace and divine purpose that my life had not been snuffed out because of my many foolish and immature decisions. He loves me and has good plans for me .

And now when I look back, several years before my first introduction to New Jerusalem Church, from time to time I would hear a certain scripture in my quiet times. Sometimes I would hear someone else talking about it or I would read it. One thing for sure, it would ALWAYS move me greatly and give me a spark of hope that the Lord still thought about me. This scripture is in Jeremiah 29:11. It reads like this:

For I know the thoughts I think toward you, says the Lord, thoughts of peace and not evil, to give you a future and a hope.

Back in those days, my former church attended a high school graduation ceremony of some of its students in Malden, Missouri. Their school choir sang a song that was written from this scripture. As I listened, I began to weep. And could not stop weeping. It became embarrassing because long after they had finished the song I was still weeping uncontrollably. Later, in retrospect, I realized that

that particular scripture presented itself to me from time to time, because it was a prelude to the restorative spiritual operations that would take place in my life to give me hope of fulfilling Destiny. Thanks be unto God! I have a future and a hope because the Lord God did not give up on me. And the good work He has begun in me, He will complete it (Philippians 1:6). Those thoughts or plans of God were from before the foundations of the world (Ephesians 1:4). And my old conscience, that is bruised, broken, and seared (1 Timothy 4:1-2) because of how I was born into this world of sin, iniquity, error, hurts, and great wounds, was going to be reckoned dead so that I could learn to walk in a new and pure one; All because Abba Father, the One true God, didn't let me go. He doesn't give up on us—even in failure, after having received His precious Holy Spirit (Ruach HaKodech) and experiencing His love, presence and power. He loves us, saves us and restores us, and even uses us to His glory because of His everlasting love and because He is not willing that any perish.

CHAPTER (19)

The "100 Life"

In the Boot Hill of Missouri, the Christian Echoes Singers was initially started by a group of mostly married women (my Mama was one of them). Not long after they started, their husbands joined them (here comes Daddy). One of the group members, a baritone singer, was Mr. Battles, but we just called him Mr. James. He used to lead the song, "Ninety-nine and a Half Won't Do." Everyone loved to hear him sing that song.

As I grow in the faith of the Lord, my question is, "Am I satisfied with that 99 and a half?" The answer is no! I ask myself, "What holds me from yielding the "100" life? What does the "100" life look like for me in the expression of Christ? And what comes with my "100" life?

Envision living a life of total dedication that pleases the Lord all the days of your life. With this kind of existence, relationship with God and others is whole and pure. The ministry of true prayer, joy, and living out God's word would increase, and whatever your ministry entails would bring God glory. Faithfulness to God, spouses and others relationships will become a norm and not an anomaly. Moreover, cooperation with the Spirit of the Lord will bring the ministry of reconciliation of souls to God and decrease the mouth of hell.

I can't help but think of the Azusa Street Revival.
Before the outpouring of God's Spirit in revival, William J.
Seymour's life was marked by hours of intense prayer
(about five hours a day). He was told that if he wanted the
breakthrough and outpouring, he had to take his prayer life
to another level. He honored that word (to seven or eight
hours a day in prayer) and God moved.

In 1906, the Azusa Street Revival was born.
Furthermore, William Seymour's intention was to restore
the faith once delivered to the saints through old-time
preaching, camp meetings, revivals, missions, street and
prison work (online information). Speaking in tongues,
faith healing, fervent prayer, emotional, from-the-heart
participatory worship and stress on evangelism became the
hallmarks of the Azusa Street experience.

I realize that while an individual's ministry through their
life span must at some point come to its end, the spirit of
true ministry should never end. Yeshua's ministry is still
going on. Some expressions of ministry are powerful,
bringing glory to God, while others need to repent and shift
in their devotion and direction.

Father Karl Barmann's expression of Christ is a
beautiful one. And he has seen the awesome overflow that
has come with the giving up of his whole life to the service
of the Lord. We are not all called to a life of celibacy as
monks or nuns, but every Christ-Believer is called to give
the Lord our all.

A scripture that I have not heard in a long time comes to
my heart right now:

*The eyes of the Lord run to and fro throughout the
whole earth to show Himself strong in the behalf of them
whose heart is perfect toward Him* (2 Chronicles 16:9).

I humbly say to the Lord, "My heart desire is to be one
of them where You look no further...if I am not up to par,
help me, transform me, make my heart pure, but look no
further."

Another scripture that comes to my heart is this;
Ephraim has mixed himself among the people, Ephraim is a cake not turned (Hosea 7:8). This speaks of consistent distractions and lukewarmness in the heart and life of the Believer. And whatever is in the heart, flows out of the life. As the half-done cake is a nauseous thing to eat, so does lukewarmness in the Believer makes the Lord want to throw up. He simply tells us that He would that we were either hot or cold for Him (Revelations 3:15).

Daniel is a prime example of the "100" life. According to the scriptures, he was one of the young princes of Jerusalem that was taken captive by the Babylonians. He was placed under the direct rule of Nebuchadnezzar as a wise man with three others, Shadrach, Meshach, and Abednego. These Babylonian names were given to them after they arrived to Babylonia. Their Hebrew names were, Hananiah, Mishael, and Azariah) And Daniel's Babylonian name was Belteshazzar.

Daniel was wise, handsome, intelligent, and was gifted by the Spirit of God, to interpret dreams. He faithfully prayed three times a day. Daniel was so graciously endowed with what God had given to him and skilled at the king's business, he was made great by King Nebuchadnezzar and given rule over the whole province of Babylon and made chief of the governors over all the wise men of Babylon, and they did not like it (Daniel 2:48). Though it was the custom of the Babylonians (or any country that took people captive) to strip their captives of their names, language and culture, Daniel was able to adjust because he had given himself wholly to the God of Abraham, Isaac and Jacob. Like Samuel, Daniel never deviated from this holy life with the Lord and was a powerful intercessor for his nation.

Jeremiah, the prophet prophesied there would be 70 years of captivity for Israel in Babylon, and it happened. But when that 70 years was fulfilled, Daniel was on the forefront to intercede to the Lord's for His hand to move on behalf of His nation for their freedom and for their return to their own land (Jeremiah 29:10-14). These men led lives entirely consecrated to the Lord. And they did not fail.

Now, I am watching and hearing our present-day leadership unveil the New Covenant that reveals the pure conscience, the faith of God and grace to live an utterly, righteous, consecrated and sanctified life, that gives me power with God, power over my own body and the ability to trust the Lord, that I too will fulfill His purpose and intent for me. Furthermore, like them by the grace of God, I will not fail because He is working in me the "100" life.

CHAPTER (20)

Not Compromising in What You Know

For as long as I have known how to read and understand, the words negotiate and compromise held two very different ends. When one negotiates something, they can work it out, thrash it out, make arrangements that they may come to an agreement that is suitable for both parties. Compromise, according to its meaning, seemed similar. *And making a compromise can mean that someone has come to an understanding.* However, for the sake of the direction of what I hope to get across, another slant of the word compromise represents some sort of fight or sharp disagreement that has to be worked through in duress. And it holds, in a general sense, a certain ring of doing something against principle or conscience. In this scenario, someone gets the short end of the stick.

When Mary, the mother of Yeshua was visited by God through the Angel Gabriel, she was told that she had found favor with God and would give birth to the Son of God. Well, she was quite astonished as to how this could take place since she was a virgin. So, she frankly asked, "How can this be since I have never 'known' or (slept with a man)?" The Angel, Gabriel replied, *"The Holy Spirit (Ruach HaKodesh) will come upon you, and the power of the Highest will overshadow you; therefore that "holy thing" which shall be born of you shall be called the Son of God* (Luke 1:30-35 kjv).

When we are born again, there is a "holy thing" in us, a new creation in Christ. That holy thing is a work of God in us, equipped with the great potential of consciousness that we could not walk in prior to our regeneration. As we grow in Christ, our pure conscience grows and starts to serve us in the places that the Lord is working on in our lives.

I shared in a previous chapter that the Lord started dealing with me way back at the beginning of my salvation experience concerning various issues. Some of these things were more difficult than others to face, but He endeavored to help me. And quite frankly, I feared, and failed to face some of those things at that time. Yet, there are places where the mark of the Hand of the Lord has touched my life and brought freedom and victory, but if I allow my fleshly humanity or that of others to take me to places *outside* of my conscience the Lord has purged, it could bring great damage to my walk with Him. This is true for any Believer. Truly, by the grace of the Lord, we prove all things.

By the grace of God, I am increasing and walking cautiously when I listen to others outside of the place the Lord has used to bring restoration in me. Too many teachers can cause confusion. A leader that reverences, cherishes and follows the Lord is more precious than silver or gold. And the Lord is able to bring us into the presence of people who will lead us in grace, truth and righteousness, and will be careful not to harm us, seeing we are the sheep of God. There may be those that we respect in this world and will listen to what they have to say. However, if something is said that does not bear witness of Christ or ring true, we don't have to throw them away, but it is best to place that thing on the back burner and pray to the Lord (even receive council with your leader) to reveal what is *behind* the things said, because what is being said may bring health, light, eternal life; or it could bring darkness, devastation, or ruin.

When we move against the pure conscience we have received, confusion will automatically come. And it is best to stop right there and cry out to the Lord, then to move on blindly into the confusion. Behind its door is never anything good. And because our conscience makes us to "know" instead of just believing, it is an assurance that should never be kicked against. When our conscience makes us to know, we are given strength to stand and not compromise.

Mary, the mother of Jesus "knew" that she had heard from God Most High about having a child when she had not been with a man sexually. She saw the Angel who came to assure her and she received grace, faith and confidence to stand when it *appeared* that she had gone astray and whoring around. She could have been stoned to death for being pregnant outside of her betrothal, (for Joseph, her betrothed, knew that _he_ hadn't been with her). She could not defend herself, thus, she was resolute that the Lord, who chose her for such an awesome task would defend and keep her so that she could fulfill her destiny. As it were, Joseph was a just man. Though he was indeed hurt over what he thought she had done, he loved her and didn't want to make a public spectacle of her. Thus, he was minded to divorce her privately (Matthew 1:19-21). Their betrothal was also considered a type of marriage, they had yet to do the ceremony before consummating it.

Furthermore, the Lord is faithful and deals with all parties, He spoke with Joseph too, but in a dream. And Joseph had to have faith in the Lord concerning this situation that was very awkward and embarrassing. Once Joseph received this acknowledgment and word, he was encouraged and strengthened and went on with plans to marry Mary. They never looked back—because they *knew*. Thus, when we know, we stand --and do not compromise our positions in the Lord. The winds of life will beat against that stand, but we must maintain and hold to the word of faith given.

John G Lake, a successful business man prior to his conversion, took a posture in his relationship with the Lord that was not easy to do at times. In his ministry along with the team that worked with him, they yielded themselves to a place of totally trusting the Lord for their lives, families and every provision. Through his ministry, thousands of people received the salvation of God; their souls saved, deliverance, provision, mercy, healing, and devils cast out. While this took place, sometimes Lake and his family and the team were in dire straits. But they continued to cry out to the Lord for their every need, and God would meet them. John Lake never asked anyone for money. And the Lord provided. Mr. Lake was known to have said these words:

"If I were to give you a watchword, it would be, "No compromise.' fight or no fight, discussion or no discussion. Principle is better than unity, and the ultimate end of principle will be oneness."
Mr. Lake never compromised his position with the Lord

Apostle/Paster C. Perry's role in my life has been that of a man of revelation, prophesy, intense prayer, power, and a loving spiritual father—indeed a man of no compromise. As the years passed, the ministry has shifted several times. I have had the honor to watch him increase in the Faith. His prayer life and model are of that which we see of the early church saints. Every shift the ministry has taken has always been for our growth within; to allow the life of the word of God to take its position as the of the line upon line and precept upon precept for the building of the Lord's life and ministry within us, and be presented in a virginal state to the Lord (2 Corinthians 11:2). We are challenged as we grow up that we might be single-minded and serious about the One who took the greatest of beatings for our iniquities, shed His blood and died, and experienced Death, Hell and the Grave. He did this to redeem the Soul. May we be cleansed of all disingenuousness towards the Lord and each other.

Apostle Perry's passion is for those God gave him, to come into the fullness of the Lord, to grow into the full stature of the Man in Christ; to live in this world and be separate, that others may see Christ in us. Some who look on our lives and see Him, will come to Him. And because of this we must not despise or compromise our new birth, which is the work of the Lord in us. May we not despise the Lord's Wisdom, Righteousness, Sanctification and Redemption whereby we are joint-partakers with Him. Furthermore, this glory whereby we are being glorified, surpasses the glory (or rags) of the world, and there is no comparison. Therefore, grace is given to us to empower us to not deviate from or compromise our conscience. It connects us with our destiny and to the end of our Faith, which is the salvation of our soul.

CHAPTER (21)

Our Appointment with God (The Clarion)

In the early hungry years (hungry for God), I took up fasting. There was a godly woman, (Darlene) in my life at that time who encouraged me along the way. She studied the word, prayed daily and fasted often. She was sent into others countries to minister and stood in the seat of a prophetess. And just by her influence, I caught the desire to fast and seek the Lord for a greater experience in Him. I tried short fasts, and long ones. I wanted the Lord to do something with me. I wanted change and the transformation that His power, presence and anointing brings, and greatly desired to be close to Him.

I remember going on my first very long fast. When I reached the middle of it, I broke it. My physical hunger just did not go away. However, I went to the Lord in repentance. He forgave me, and I strongly felt I was to resume the fast. So, I did. He graciously helped me to complete it. The same thing happened on another long fast. Yet, again, the Lord helped me to complete that one too. Now, in this present time, I sense the Hand of the Lord and His wooing Presence again. And I know it's not just me.

Sometimes we resist the nudging to pray. And I assure you, it is not our humanity that is nudging. It is the wooing of the Almighty to come and spend time with Him. It is His gentle Presence that moves upon us to come and sit and be still so He can speak, have fellowship with us and give guidance. Yet we may resist and find something else to occupy that time and make excuses as to why we cannot do it.

We make appointments for all sorts of reasons; doctor, veterinarian, dentist, job interviews, parents and teacher. But for some reason, when it is time for our appointment with the Lord, He is left out. It is not for His good that He calls us, it is for ours. He doesn't really need us (though He loves us and chooses to use us), but *we do need Him*. Yet we may behave as if He is on our string when we want something or an emergency comes up.

We actually live in the most urgent times and need to know in whom we believe. Our anchor must be fixed in the Lord. Our hope must be fixed in Him. Our lives must be built in Him, the Rock, so that our house won't fall flat during the torrential storms of life (Matthew 7:24-27). The only way to that place with Him is through prayer and the truth of His word.

The Lord is calling us to allow Him to set an appointment with Him and for us to keep it. We cannot blame Him for the things that goes sideways in our lives. Even if we think we are not to blame for our problems, we have a God who sees, hears, knows and answers us. Thus, we have to look within to see what hinders us. We can see the outside, but it is not necessarily the outside that stops us. We stop ourselves...from within!

The Greatest of all, the glorious Champion of Love wants *us*, (when others didn't or don't want us) and when we obediently answer His call, He will help us deal with those impediments, and will soon crush Satan under our feet (Romans 16:19-20).

TO THE READER: THE CALL...

Thank you for choosing to pick up this writing and deciding to read its pages. I pray it has yielded some light of God and gives insight, hope, and brings life and restorative beginnings.

To Believers in Christ Jesus (Yeshua): To those who have been in ministry and have walked with God **(YHWH)**, these writings speak to us.

Maybe there are those of you who have struggled with having shipwrecked your life; shipwrecked in the faith? Perhaps even made mockery of God by trampling under foot His blood sacrifice? Maybe you have enjoyed His abundant grace, partaken of His mercy, goodness, and kindness, then turned your back on Him?

This also speaks to those who have received healing in body, words of faith, knowledge and Wisdom that took you to the next level and you fell from that place?

Additionally, perhaps you may have been used mightily in the Ministry of the Lord and walked unworthy of that ministry? Or in a lukewarm state?

To all of this I say, Brother and Sister, turn to Him and find your altar again and pray. His holy word encourages and comforts us by revealing that *where sin abounds, grace does much more abound* (Romans 5:20-21).

If you are beaten to a pulp by guilt and shame and have no hope, return to the safety of His Arms, Face, His Bosom of warmth, intimacy and love and ministry, because there is hope. Return to the Lord…and pray. *For whosoever shall call upon the name of the Lord shall be saved* (Romans 10:13).

The Lord never gave up on you. He did not cast you aside. Let me freely tell you the truth: He _does_ chastise those He loves (and He loves you). And we _do_ reap what we sow; but that is not His fault! So then we must first look in the mirror, truly see ourselves and acknowledge what we see.

Furthermore, I have some more good news: You can be restored. Can you believe it? He does love you. Can you truly believe that? Let prayer begin in you again. Reach out to Him and find the place of repentance. Believe into Him. Trust that He is not like our humanity, which is fickle, unfaithful and untrustworthy, or like a see saw, up one moment and down the next. Believe that if you truly repent, He forgives you and He will not hold a grudge against you.

The songwriter, _Will L. Thompson_ wrote a hymn called, "Softly and Tenderly." It goes like this:

Softly and tenderly Jesus is calling, calling for you and for me.
See on the portals He's waiting and watching, Watching for you and for me.
Come home, come home. Ye who are weary come home
Earnestly, tenderly Jesus is calling, calling oh, sinner (oh, lost saints) come home

The father of the prodigal ran to welcome his son, who, after a long time came home after only-God-knows-where he had been and what he had done (Luke 15:11-32). Is not the Almighty, greater than the father of the prodigal? Isn't the prodigal's forgiving father God's creation? Yes, he is! And Heavenly Father is greater and more merciful. Truly, His arms are also open wide and He is running to you welcoming you back home. Come Home! Come home wounded soldier. Come home lost saint. Come home sinner. Come Home.

ABOUT THE AUTHOR

Dr. Purity M Williams is the founder of New School Bus Creation Music, Ministry & Publishing (in association with, The Intercessor's Room) in Springfield, MO. She is a singer, songwriter, musician, and a missionary to several countries in Russia: (Moscow, Odinsovo, Yegoryevsk); East Africa: (Kenya, Uganda, Tanzania); and Central Africa: (Democratic Republic of Congo, Lubumbashi, Mbuji-Mayi, Mwene-ditu) and Thailand.

She attended Evangel University, Central Bible College, Three Rivers Community College, World Vision School of Missions, Hannibal LaGrange University, International College of Bible Theology, Mt Calvary Power House School of Prophets, and Midwest Seminary of Bible Theology obtaining an Associates in General Education, Two-year Diploma for Missions Training, Bachelor of Ministry, Bachelor of Science in Organizational Management, a Master of Arts in Leadership (Christian Ministry emphasis), and a Doctor of Biblical Studies (Christian Ministry, Teaching & Preaching emphasis) and certification in Chaplaincy.

Purity has been in ministry for over 30 years. At the onset of her new birth, her heart was and yet is for people to experience the salvation of the Lord, to be reconciled to God and trained to know His word, to understand and know their new birth, the New Covenant, and the God who provided it, and lastly, they grow up in Christ. Prayer is her heart and exhortation. It is a door to knowing the Lord and understanding His Word. It is a door to healing, deliverance, revelation, and restoration for the unregenerate, the new believer, the old believer, and the backslider or one who truly desires to come back to the Lord.

Dr. Purity Williams currently resides in Springfield, MO. She has precious and lovely children: Jin, Frederick, Sara, and her beautiful grandchildren: Trinity, Deldrick Jr., Cooper (Bruce), and Tiannah.

REFERENCES

Abarem Publications. (2022). [article]. Jericho Meaning. Jericho | The amazing name Jericho: meaning and etymology (abarim-publications.com)

Barmann. K. Rev. (2023). [Interview]. His Discipline: 43 Years of Service to God as a Benedictine Priest/Monk and an Air Force Chaplain (Combined).

Bunyan, J. (1998). [Book]. The Pilgrim's Progress. (In Modern English).Revised by L. Edward Hazelbaker. Bridge-Logos Publishing. Alachua, Florida.

Burchette, S. (2020). The Role of Timothy and Titus: Apostolic Representatives, Not Pastors. Christian Communicators Worldwide. The Role of Timothy and Titus: Apostolic Representatives, Not Pastors - CCW - Christian Communicators Worldwide (ccwtoday.org)

Cherry, K. (2022). [article]. What is the Difference Between Conscience and Conscious? https://www.verywellmind.com/conscience-vs-conscious-whats-the-difference-2794961

Ciampaglia, D. (2018-2019). [article]. Why Were Vietnam Vets Treated Poorly When They Returned? Why Vietnam War Vets Were Treated Poorly When They Returned - HISTORY

Cloud, D. (2022). The Christian Soldier. The Way of Life Literature.

Dirt Connections. (2022) [article]. Pros and Cons of Tilling Soil (dirtconnections.com)

Goff, P. (2019). [article]. Why Can't Science Explain Consciousness? It's the Greatest Challenge of Our Time. https://www.livescience.com/what-is-consciousness-mystery.html

Hebrew Word Studies Index, Greek Word Studies Index. (2022). HEBREW WORD STUDIES on חֵן 'chen' meaning 'Grace' 2580 (logosapostolic.org)

Infantado. Joshua. (2017). Three Effective Ways On

How We Can Examine Ourselves. Becoming Christians. 3 Effective Ways on How We can Examine Ourselves | Becoming Christians

Insight State. (2023). 12 Types of Spiritual Practices. List of 12 Types of Spiritual Practices. 12 Types Of Spiritual Practices - Insight state

Jewish Public Society. (1999). [Book]. Hebrew-English TANAKH. The Jewish Publication Society, Philadelphia 1999.

Jewish.Shop. (2022). [article]. Back to Jewish. What Does Covenant Mean In Hebrew? What Does Covenant Mean In Hebrew? » Jewish.Shop

Jewish Virtual Library. (1998-2023). [article]. Barrenness and Fertility. Jewish Virtual Library. A Project of AICE. Barrenness and Fertility (jewishvirtuallibrary.org)

Johnson, E. [Interview]. (2022). And Written Narrative of 10 Years of Service in the United States Army

Knox, A. (2008). [article]. The Assembling of the Church. Was Timothy the Bishop of Ephesus? | The Assembling of the Church (alanknox.net)

Kroll. P. (2023). [article]. Church History: William Seymour and the Rise of Pentecostalism. Grace Community International. William Seymour and the Rise of Pentecostalism - Grace Communion International (gci.org)

McMinn, M. (2008). [Book]. Sin And Grace: in Christian Counseling. InterVarsity Press. P.O. Box 1400, Downers Grove, IL.

Mcquillen, H. (2022). [article]. What were the awards given in the Ancient Olympics? What Were the Awards Given in the Ancient Olympics? - Sportsmanist

Military.com. (2023). 6 Things To Know About Operation Desert Storm. 6 Things to Know About Operation Desert Storm | Military.com

Military One Source. (2022). [article]. Military Special Forces: Navy SEALs, Green Berets & More • Military

OneSource

Military Spot.com. (2004-2023). [article]. Understanding the Five Branches of the Military. Understanding the Five Branches of the Military - MilitarySpot.com

Morin, A. LCSW. (2017). [article]. 10 Signs You're A People-Pleaser: You'll Never Reach Your Goals If You're Trying To Be All Things To All People. Psychology Today. 10 Signs You're a People-Pleaser | Psychology Today

Murray, A. (2022). [article]. The Husbandman. The Mystery of the True Vine. The Husbandman, The Mystery of the True Vine, Andrew Murray, Christian Classics books at BibleStudyTools.com

National Institute of Mental Health. 2022. Mental Health Information. NIMH » Post-Traumatic Stress Disorder (nih.gov)

New King James Bible (internet). https://www.biblegateway.com/passage/?search=1+Cori nthians+13%3A1-8&version=NIV;NKJV

OMK. (2023). [article]. Coast Guard Special Forces. 5 Coast Guard Special Forces You (probably) Never Heard Of (operationmilitarykids.org)

Perry, C. A. (2015-2023). Prayer, The Power of the Purged Conscience, Grace & Truth, and Foundational Teachings from various services.

The Prayer Pocket. (2022). 10 Benefits of Prayer.10 Benefits Of Prayer – (theprayerpocket.com).

Przybylski. D. (2013). [article]. The Overflow of the Consecrated Life. Crosswalk.com. The Overflow of a Consecrated Life (crosswalk.com)

Reidt, W. (1989). [Book]. John G. Lake: A Man Without Compromise. Harrison House Publisher 1989.

Religions. (2021). learnreligions.com/timothy-companion-of-the-apostle-paul-701073.

Roland, J. (2022). [article]. The Power of the Focused

Life. The Power of a Focused Life - Jen Roland
Rouse. B. (2004). Book). The Little Foxes; Things
Christians Do Not Have To Do. AuthorHouse. 04/07/2004.
Bloomington, Indiana US.
Salt and Light Ministries. (2019). [article]. Total
Commitment to God (Part 1). TOTAL COMMITMENT
TO GOD (PART 1) – Salt and Light Ministries
(saltandlightministriesgh.org)
Secret Church. (2016). Radical. What Does Jainism
Teach? What Does Jainism Teach? - Radical.
Sherman, F. (2018). [article]. If a Soldier Wants to Quit
at Boot Camp, Will the Arm Just Release Him? CHRON. If
a Soldier Wants to Quit at Boot Camp, Will the Army Just
Release Him? (chron.com)
Seymour. W. J. (2014). The 100 Year Prophesy. 100
Year Prophecy (William J Seymour) - Bing video
SOFREP. (2021). [article]. US Army Special Forces
"Green Berets" The Complete Guide. US Army Special
Forces "Green Berets" | The Complete Guide | SOFREP
United States Code. (2011). Edition. Title 10 ARMED
FORCES. Enlistment Oath. U.S.C. Title 10 - ARMED
FORCES (govinfo.gov)
Upcouncel Technologies, Inc., (2020). [article]
Difference Between Covenant and Contract. Difference
Between Covenant and Contract (upcounsel.com)
URI. (2023). [article]. Buddhism: Basic Beliefs | URI
USMILITARY.COM. (2022). [article]. How to Become
a Night Stalker in the Army. How to Become a Night
Stalker in the Army - US Military
White, M. M.A. (2023). 5 Main World Religions and
Their Basic Beliefs. 5 Main World Religions and Their
Basic Beliefs | YourDictionary
Wilkes, C. G. (1998). (Book). Jesus On Leadership:
Timeless Wisdom on Servant Leadership. Lifeway Press.
1998 Tyndale House Publishers. Carole Stream, Illinois
60188.

Yap, V. (2005) [article]. Everything To Prove. Everything To Prove Sermon by Victor Yap, 1 Kings 11:42-12:20 - SermonCentral.com

Zavada, Jack. (2021). "Meet Timothy: Protege of the Apostle Paul."

Made in the USA
Monee, IL
24 December 2023

49220331R00090